PASSWORDS TO A HAPPY LIFE

Also by Sirshree

Spiritual Masterpieces - Self Realisation books for serious seekers

Who Am I Now: From mindfulness to no-mind
Answers that Awaken: Access the Source of Wisdom within You
100% Karma: Learn the Art of Conscious Karma that Liberates
100% Wisdom: Wisdom that leads you to experience and be established in your true nature
100% Meditation: Dip into the Stillness of Pure Awareness
You are Meditation: Discover Peace and Bliss Within
Essence of Devotion: From Devotee to Divinity
The Unshaken Mind: Discovering the Purpose, Power and Potential of your mind
The Supreme Quest: Your search for the Truth ends there where you are
The Greatest Freedom: Discover the key to an Awakened Living
Secret of The Third Side of The Coin: Unravelling Missing Links in Spirituality
Seek Forgiveness & be Free: Liberation from Karmic Bondage

Self Help Treasures - Self Development books for success seekers

The Source of Health: The Key to Perfect Health Discovery
Inner Ninety Hidden Infinity: How to build your book of values
Inner 90 for Youth: The secret of reaching and staying at the peak of success
The Source for Youth: You have the power to change your life
Inner Magic: The Power of self-talk
Self Encounter: The Complete Path - Self Development to Self Realization
The Five Supreme Secrets of Life: Unveiling the Ways to Attain Wealth, Love and God
You are Not Lazy: A story of shifting from Laziness to Success
Freedom From Fear, Worry, Anger: How to be cool, calm and courageous
The Little Gita of Problem Solving: Gift of 18 Solutions to Any Problem
Freedom From Failure: 7 Spiritual Secrets That Transform Failure Into A Blessing

New Age Nuggets - Practical books on applied spirituality and self help

The Source: Power of Happy Thoughts
Secret of Happiness: Instant Happiness - Here and Now!
Excuse me God...: Fulfilling your wishes through the Power of Prayer and Seed of Faith
Help God to Help You: Whatever you do, do it with a smile
Ultimate Purpose of Success: Achieving Success in all five aspects of life
Celebrating Relationships: Bringing Love, Life, Laughter in Your Relations
Everything is a Game of Beliefs: Understanding is the Whole Thing
Detachment From Attachment: Gift of Freedom From Suffering
Emotional Freedom Through Spiritual Wisdom: How to Take Charge of Your Emotions

Profound Parables - Fiction books containing profound truths

Beyond Life: Conversations on Life After Death
The One Above: What if God was your neighbour?
The Warrior's Mirror: The Path To Peace
Master of Siddhartha: Revealing the Truth of Life and After-life
Put Stress to Rest: Utilizing Stress to Make Progress
The Source @ Work: A Story of Inspiration from Jeeodee

The Art of Being
Happy in all Situations

PASSWORDS TO A HAPPY LIFE

Author of the bestseller *The Source*

SIRSHREE

PASSWORDS TO A HAPPY LIFE

The Art of Being Happy in all Situations

By Sirshree Tejparkhi

Copyright © Tejgyan Global Foundation
All Rights Reserved 2018

Tejgyan Global Foundation is a charitable organization with its headquarters in Pune, India.

Published by WOW Publishings Pvt. Ltd., India

First edition published in June 2018

Printed and bound by Repro India Limited
This book is based on the Hindi book - Sukhi Jeevan ke Password

Copyrights are reserved with Tejgyan Global Foundation and publishing rights are vested exclusively with WOW Publishings Pvt. Ltd. This book is sold subject to the condition that it shall not by way of trade or otherwise, be lent, resold, hired out, or otherwise circulated without the publisher's prior written consent in any form of binding or cover other than that in which it is published and without a similar condition including this condition being imposed on the subsequent purchaser and without limiting the rights under copyright reserved above, no part of this publication may be reproduced, stored in or introduced into a retrieval system, or transmitted, in any form, or by any means, electronic, mechanical, photocopying, recording or otherwise, without the prior written permission of both the copyright owner and the above-mentioned publisher of this book. Any person who does any unauthorized act in relation to this publication may be liable to criminal prosecution and civil claims for damages.

To those
who became an inspiration for others
by leading a happy life themselves.

Contents

Preface		9

THE PASSWORD HIDDEN IN THE CAVE OF THE MIND

1.	Flowers hidden in the dust	15
2.	The Cave of Negative Emotions	18
3.	How to Pass through the Tunnels of Emotions?	21

THE SEVEN PASSWORDS TO A HAPPY LIFE

4.	The First Password to a Happy Life	27
5.	Unhappiness - A Reminder and Feedback	30
6.	Tell Nature what you are in Favor of	34
7.	Stop Negative Affirmations	38
8.	The Second Password to a Happy Life	41
9.	Learn your Lessons from your Partner	45
10.	Safeguard your Diamonds	49
11.	The Third Password to a Happy Life	52
12.	The Truth Hides behind your Illusion	61

13.	Two Principles of Life – Illusion and the Bright Truth	69
14.	The Fourth Password to a Happy Life	74
15.	The Fifth Password to a Happy Life	80
16.	The Sixth Password to a Happy Life	87
17.	The Seventh Password to a Happy Life	92

THE LOCK OF SORROW AND DISTRESS

18.	Cause 1: Separation from God	97
19.	Cause 2: The Habit of Dwelling in Sorrow	100
20.	Cause 3: Are we Unhappy about Others' Happiness?	104
21.	Cause 4: Feeling Unhappy about Unhappiness	110
22.	Cause 5: Forgetting the True Purpose of Life	116
23.	Cause 6: Actions backed by Ignorance	120
24.	Cause 7: The Restlessness of the Mind	124

APPENDIX

Preface

Seek Happiness within

For the moment, imagine that you're passionate about the taste of chocolate. But, from where you live, it's not easy to get. In fact, you need to travel quite a distance to get chocolate. It's nearly impossible to reach a satisfying supply.

One day you get word that a cave on a nearby mountain is full of chocolate. There's only one catch – there's an active volcano on the mountain. You wake up one morning and decide can't wait any longer, you're going to face the potential danger of climbing that mountain.

As luck would have it, when you're climbing the mountain the lava that rises from the volcano falls upon you, scalding your skin. You're in extreme pain, but when you look at your skin, to your utter surprise, you find chocolate inside those spots where your skin got charred!

You stumbled upon the secret that you're made of chocolate. You're made of the very thing that you were seeking all this while!

All through our lives, we seek happiness in external pursuits of the world. We get deluded by daily life situations. We seek relief to our problems by taking refuge in knowledge that is based on false beliefs and by succumbing to the lures of the material world.

When we derive happiness through some external means, we create a formula and try to repeat the same formula hoping to get the same result time after time. The same formula doesn't necessarily bring happiness every time. And our incessant search for happiness goes on.

Some people resort to chanting, meditation, penance, devotion and other austerities to experience happiness. But even these well-meaning activities don't yield everlasting happiness.

Happiness seems so elusive. The more people you talk to the more you discover that happiness doesn't appear to be the norm. Regardless of their income, the number of worldly items they've accumulated, they aren't happy.

They flit from one item to another, they try to make themselves happy through other means, including pills, food, shopping and any other method you could think of.

Why are human beings cursed with this seemingly inherent lack of happiness? Have we been seeking happiness at the wrong places? What if you were told that we have cursed ourselves with regards to our joy? What if you were told that with seven easy passwords, you can enter the world of happiness, not just for five minutes, five days or even five months?

Happiness can be yours every single day for the rest of your life, with the aid of these seven passwords. These passwords, when used properly can flip your perspective on your emotions. No longer will sorrow or suffering be your "default" response or "default" emotion.

Just like the chocolate, you're made of the thing that you were seeking all the time. If you're told that happiness lies within you and you are, indeed, made up of happiness at your core, how will you lead your life?

You'll start from where you stand right now. Do this and all through the journey of life, you'll be happy and content at the start, in the middle and in the end of the journey.

You'll discover that there is no way to happiness; rather, happiness itself is the way. With this understanding, you'll find that you have already arrived! You'll no longer depend on external situations to make you happy. Instead, your inherent happiness will trigger a radical change not only within you but around you as well. Your happy state will attract good health, harmonious relationships, prosperity and success in your life.

In the forthcoming sections of this book, you'll receive the seven passwords to a happy life, which you can use to easily access the treasure trove of happiness. You'll then witness how these passwords can create miracles in your life.

Armed with this amazing knowledge, you'll know the true causes of unhappiness and how to remedy them in the form of these passwords. You will realize the secret of a happy life, which transcends both joy and sorrow.

So, grab a box of chocolates, sit back and read how to achieve everlasting happiness.

SECTION I

THE PASSWORD HIDDEN IN THE CAVE OF THE MIND

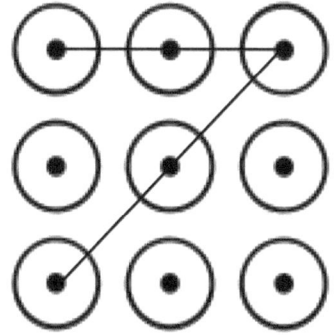

1
Flowers hidden in the dust

Increasingly, our lives seem to be dominated by knowing the right passwords. This is especially if you spend any time at all on the internet. You need the correct password for all your social media sites, for your online bank accounts and even for stray sites that don't seem worthy of a password-guarded entrance.

So, you may sigh and even groan to think about another password. But if seven passwords could unlock the key to happiness, wouldn't it be at least worth thinking about. The guaranteed advantage to these passwords is that once you learn them, you'll never need to change them.

Consider the following two phrases and reflect on which one you will choose.

1. No one should misunderstand me.

2. May I attain complete freedom from bondage and unhappiness.

If you end up choosing the first one, then attaining complete freedom is not a priority for you. All that you desire is that people should not misunderstand you.

If you do choose the second phrase, you will get the passwords to a happy life. The seven passwords for a happy life have been detailed in further chapters. You may find these passwords very ordinary to begin with, but if you apply them diligently in your day-to-day life, your life will blossom with love, joy and complete and continuous peace.

Before learning about the seven passwords, though, let's understand how people complicate their lives by getting stuck in their bad habits, tendencies, negative thoughts and emotions. Getting free of bondage to attain freedom then becomes nothing more than an unreachable goal. Love, joy and peace remain far-off ideals. But when they gain understanding and free themselves from tendencies, negative thoughts and emotions, they lead a joyful life.

The analogy below sheds some light on this:

Imagine you are traveling in a car up a mountain which has a flat land at the top. On the way to the mountain top, your car travels through several small tunnels.

After passing through several tunnels, you reach a check-post at the end, where the amount of dust accumulated on your car is checked. Most of the people do not clean their cars throughout their journey. Very few people clean their cars every now and then. While passing through the tunnels, if the cars come to a standstill due to traffic, some people get out and sketch various floral designs on the layer of accumulated dust on their cars.

Those vehicles with very little dust are the only ones that are permitted to continue on from the check-post. The cars that possess a thick layer of dust are sent back down through another route. They're not permitted to go to the summit. Each car is also equipped with a recording facility. As soon as the car passes through a tunnel, the recording equipment switches on. It records all the thoughts and the chatter going on in your mind while passing through the tunnel.

Each tunnel is distinct and causes a distinct set of thoughts in your mind. You notice a board at every tunnel. Something is written on each board, however since it's in a foreign language, you are unable to decipher it. The recorder chronicles the ongoing chatter of your mind.

The check-post also checks the recording of each car and decides if the passenger should be sent ahead or asked to turn back. People have different reactions to their recordings at the check-post. Some people complain, like, "The roads were bad… The climate was miserable… There was so much dust… There was a storm… What was my mistake…?"

There's a long queue at the check-post. While waiting for their turn, some people get out of their car and continue to sketch floral designs in the accumulated dust on their cars. Some keep complaining while others keep drawing beautiful designs on the dust.

Think about who will be sent ahead to the mountain top. Those who complained all the time or those who sketched floral designs? What was the understanding and the life-experience of those who complained? What was the understanding and wisdom possessed by those who sketched floral designs? To know the answers to all these aspects, stay through the journey of this book, so that you are able to know all the facets of this analogy.

Let's understand more in the next chapter…

2
The Cave of Negative Emotions

The analogy given in the previous chapter had a very deep meaning hidden in it. If you are able to grasp its subtlety, you will be free of suffering and lead a joyful life filled with love. Let's understand the deeper essence of this analogy now.

The significance of the symbols –

- The car – The human body made of the five fundamental elements

- The accumulated layer of dust – Our patterns, habitual tendencies, and deep-seated beliefs

- The tunnel – The negative emotions arising within our mind

- The check-post – Karmic accounts (the law of nature)

- The road leading to the mountain – Rising to the highest state of consciousness

- The road leading back down – Falling prey to the illusory world

- The flat land at the top – The space for the highest creation from the standpoint of pure consciousness.

◆ Recording – Negative programming imprinted in the memory

Every person on Earth can attempt to fulfil the highest goal of life: "To experientially know who we truly are through Self-realization and abide in that ultimate blissful state referred to as Self-stabilization."

However, man gets deluded in the material world of illusions and forgets his true life purpose. He believes himself to be a limited body-mind and gets trapped in its patterns, tendencies and beliefs, thus compelling himself to possibly even lead a miserable life.

The Journey of the Car: The Body

Man sets out on his journey towards the highest level of consciousness in his car, i.e., in his body, where the highest expression of the Self occurs. The potential is to be a part of this ultimate expression at the highest level of consciousness.

During this journey, he needs to pass through several tunnels representing the different emotions arising in his mind. However, due to a lack of understanding, he gets stuck in them. His patterns, wrong habits and tendencies don't allow him to progress any further. As a result, instead of moving along on his journey to the next stage of consciousness, he falls back.

If he attains the wisdom what thoughts he must keep and how he must watch them while passing through the tunnels of his emotions, he can easily pass through the tunnels and reach the highest level of consciousness. There, he becomes free of all suffering and attains the state of ultimate bliss beyond both happiness and sorrow.

On the contrary, if he complains, whines and blames others while traversing through the tunnel of his emotions, he continues to lead an unhappy life.

While driving, he comes to the front of a cave, Here, he sees a tunnel leading through it, symbolizing the state of his body and mind. When different emotions arise in him, he easily senses the changes happening in his body and falsely believes that the emotions have arisen in his body. The emotions have actually arisen in his mind, not body. But he can't recognize that. In a very real sense, he is actually traveling through the inner cave of his mind.

The symbolic reference made to the "foreign language on the board" refers to the language of emotions and feelings. Since we don't understand our emotions or feelings, for the most part it might as well be viewed as a foreign language. When emotions surface in our body-mind, we feel unhappy and our mind starts the chatter of negative thoughts.

We're unable to express what we feel. Because of this, we procrastinate and divert our attention to something else, anything else. In this way we believe we're bypassing these negative emotions. Sometimes, we express our disappointment by getting irritated or picking a fight. If our mind doesn't feel gratified in doing that, it seeks refuge in some addiction to surpass it.

Addictions aren't just limited to those that immediately come to mind – smoking, drinking or drugs. It could also manifest as indulgence in excessive shopping, eating or other forms of material entertainment. Although initially, we may feel relieved from our emotions. But it's nothing more than a temporary remedy. In fact, you'd have a difficult time calling it a remedy at all. It's just an escape. It works in the complete opposite way that many may have intended it to. In the long run, instead of freeing ourselves from our emotions, we get trapped in their whirlpool and further get mired in their quicksand.

3

How to Pass through the Tunnels of Emotions?

Man is always faced with the storm of his emotions and feelings. With every incident, every interaction, good or bad emotions arise within his mind. If someone says something hurtful to him, he feels heaviness in his heart. If there is a feeling of fear, he senses pressure in his stomach. The burden of responsibilities shows its effect on his shoulders and back. He doesn't feel good in any way. To escape these negative feelings and seek temporary relief, his mind fixes the blame on other people or indulges in unnecessary churning and chatter. Let's understand this through an example.

Imagine that several unexpected guests arrive at your home at midnight. Unwillingly, you put up a mask of false happiness and invite them with a fake smile. Although, you offer them food and tea, you are seething within, "Shouldn't they have some common sense… How can they just show up at someone's place so late in the night? Is this the time to go to anyone's house? I am already so tired and there is so much to do! Now, I need to tend to their needs!"

In this way, the mind churns and chatters! In the above example, you grumble within, yet you keep up the farce of being hospitable and inviting. These two opposites are at odds within you. While you may not always be able to influence the external fact (of guests showing up), if you choose to, you can very well change whatever is going on within you.

Your positive and negative mental reactions are your karma at the subtle emotional level. Hence, it's essential to understand your emotions. If you can do this, then you will keep the right thoughts while passing through the tunnel of emotions.

Only right thoughts can create a transformation in your life.

Otherwise, you won't be allowed to proceed further on your journey due to this constant chatter of your mind; you will be sent back.

Have you ever wondered what exactly is being recorded in the vehicle of your body-mind while passing through the journey of life? Whatever has been recorded so far while passing through various tunnels, is it troubling you or helping you to become free? The day you will learn to pass through these tunnels with wisdom, it will be a memorable day, indeed. Let's understand more through an example.

There was a shopkeeper. He had a small shop and earned enough to barely live on. Despite this he was happy and satisfied with his means. However, one day he came to know that a supermarket was opening opposite his small shop. He became tense and began to lament, "Who will buy from my small shop when such a huge supermarket is coming up... My shop's location is wrong.... My shop is useless.... Now my business will be ruined... Why do such things happen only to me? Now what will happen to me and my family... What harm have I caused to anyone for this to happen with me..."

Finally, in this state of emotional turmoil, he approached his spiritual teacher and narrated everything to him. He asked his guru, "Please advise me what should I do?"

The guru replied, "Every morning when you go for your morning walk, pass through your shop and pause for some time. Stand in front of your shop, watch it with love and seek forgiveness from it."

This surprised the shopkeeper, "But why should I seek forgiveness from my shop?"

The guru replied, "Because it has helped you earn your living, fed you and your family for years. Yet, you've harbored negative thoughts about your shop like it is useless and have never thanked it in all this time. Thus, mentally seek forgiveness from your shop by saying, 'Please forgive me.'"

"But, the shop is a non-living thing. How will this make a difference?" asked the perplexed shopkeeper.

"Your shop may not be 'living,' but your thoughts are very much alive. They live within you. The actual attempt here is to heal your thoughts about your shop. Trust me, and use the daily ritual of your morning walk as an opportunity to cleanse your thoughts."

"Not just this, in the same vein, you must also seek forgiveness from the supermarket by saying, 'Please forgive me for harboring negative thoughts about you… I hated you… I wished ill for you… Please forgive me for my wrongdoing.'"

Although he didn't fully understand the logic behind seeking forgiveness from non-living things, he began doing it anyway because of his faith on his guru.

After a month, he reported back to his teacher, "Revered guru, I am closing down my shop." The guru asked, "Why? What happened?" The shopkeeper answered happily, "I have been offered to run the supermarket coming up opposite my shop." The guru wondered with a smile, "So, how do you think this miracle happened?"

He replied, "Every morning I would go for my morning walk, and as you had instructed, I sought forgiveness from the supermarket as well as my shop and even thanked them. The owner of the supermarket also used to come for a walk and we became friends. One day as I paused my walk and sought forgiveness in front of my shop, he asked me what I was doing. Because we'd become friends, I narrated everything. He loved the reasoning and told me, 'Because of your polite and truthful nature, and your experience of running your shop for so many years, I offer you the job of running the supermarket.'"

"So, what did you learn? That you should make friends? That you should use your morning walk to make friends? Exactly, what is the lesson here?"

"No", said the shopkeeper to the satisfaction of his teacher, "The biggest lesson is to transform my thoughts. We would have never become friends in the first place had I continued to harbor negative thoughts. Forgiveness helped me hold my concern for competition lightly and filled my heart with warmth. That's the key."

This is the miracle of forgiveness! Shift from berating to celebrating... Transform your bemoaning to blossoming! Let the flowers of gratitude and forgiveness blossom in your heart to make you a magnet of politeness and positivity.

If man has received the wisdom of truth and is equipped with the right understanding and discerning power, he'll make the right use of wisdom while passing through every tunnel. Not only this, but he will also utilize this wisdom to better his life and progress to higher levels of consciousness - the very purpose of life. Elevate to higher levels instead of staying entangled in tunnels.

SECTION II

THE SEVEN PASSWORDS TO A HAPPY LIFE

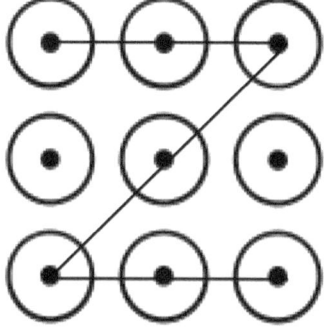

4

The First Password to a Happy Life

Whenever you are unhappy, you pass through a tunnel called Distress. Unhappiness is the first tunnel. However, as you were ignorant that this is merely a tunnel that has arisen in your journey, you kept churning your thoughts of unhappiness. And this repeated emotion was imprinted in the recording machine of your body-mind.

Whenever you affirm to yourself phrases like, "I am stressed… I am distressed… I am angry… I am troubled… I am getting bored… I hate people…," you are actually forgetting your true nature and drifting into negativity. Instead of doing that, remind yourself, "What is the truth and who am I in reality? Do my emotions define who I truly am or am I something else?" The password to a Happy Life is related with this.

The deepest and the most core belief everyone holds onto is, "I am the body." Man believes himself to be the body and leads his life in suffering by getting stuck in the game play of happiness and sorrow. However, when he reaches the peak of suffering, where he can no longer endure the pain of suffering, certain questions surface in his mind: "Is this the way to lead life and ultimately pass on from Earth? Why have I come on Earth? Why do I exist? Who am I?" This leads him in his search for the truth. His search for the truth is initiated, then, because of suffering. In that sense, the suffering that propels him forward to seeking truth is not really suffering.

Suffering gives us the first password to a Happy Life, "Who am I?" This is the first password of all mankind.

No animal will ever have this question because it doesn't need it and neither does it have the intelligence to think about it. Man has the ability to think and can understand this question. The moment he says, "I am distressed," he can use the first password and ask himself, "Who was distressed? Who am I? When I say I am distracted, who exactly is this 'I'?" Next time you are unhappy, do not fail to use this password. Use the first password to shift from the negative emotion as follows. "Hmmm… I say I am unhappy. So, who am I? Am I the emotion of unhappiness? Or am I the carrier of the emotion? **Who I truly am is a peaceful being who is currently passing through the tunnel of an emotion called unhappiness.**" Thus, your recording can completely change with the first password. The question, "Who am I?" becomes a bridge for you to notice who you are is an existential being currently passing through the tunnel of a negative emotion. Like how a train passes through a tunnel, you too are currently passing through, or having, a negative emotion. Who you actually are is in the "light" of peace and tend to pass through small tunnels of distress intermittently.

When you are ill, you are actually passing through the tunnel of illness, but you tend to say, "I am ill." However, you should say, "I am the epitome of health and wellness, who is now passing through the tunnel of illness."

The understanding here is to realize that illness is not permanent and just deal it as you deal with the pimples on your face. Several such pimples come and go. Otherwise, the more you keep thinking that you are ill or unhealthy, you are actually affirming a lie to nature. Nature grants you your fruits according to your belief

People forget who they truly are in the face of suffering and distress. If you are able to remember yourself, you will tell yourself, "I am a being, usually happy, who is now passing through a small tunnel of suffering." This will help you to ride over the unnecessary pain. You'll then continue your journey towards a joyful life.

Have you ever said, "I am a happy person" when you are in pain?

Starting today, use the first password to switch to positive affirmations. Shift from suffering to surfing in happiness. This is because suffering has actually helped you realize your true nature and thus suffering is not suffering; suffering is a reminder; suffering is a feedback; it is a divine call for you to awaken.

You can buy the ticket for a show that's sold out at a higher price on the black market, that is, through unofficial channels. What is the need to solicit unhappiness at a bloated price illicitly? When you are mired in unhappiness, this is what you are doing - purchasing suffering in the black market at a significantly higher cost. As you hold on to your belief that suffering is "you", you continue to record and imprint unhappiness. As a result, your car was sent back down instead of journeying further towards the flat land on the mountain. As such, there is no suffering. You are passing through a temporary tunnel of unhappiness.

You must learn to open this lock of unhappiness with the right password, so that the path to a happy life can open up for you.

5

Unhappiness - A Reminder and Feedback

In the beginning of this book, you were given two statements to choose one from –

1. No one should misunderstand me.

2. May I gain complete freedom from bondage and unhappiness, even if I am misunderstood by people.

Most people choose the first statement. We deeply desire that people should not misunderstand us. However, let's look at an example where this desire leads us to.

There is a graveyard in a village. It has different sections. Whenever someone dies in the village, his or her dead body is buried in one of those sections based on the way they lived their life.

The first section is reserved for those who said "I am right" and spent their entire life in an attempt to prove themselves so. The epitaph inscribed on their gravestone reads, "Here lies a man who was always right… but always unhappy."

The epitaph inscribed on the gravestones of those in the second section reads, "Here lies a man who was always wrong… but always remained happy." This is at least better than the one in the first section. This category of people rejoiced while living. Others rejected and criticized them, but they weren't the least bit bothered. They lived and died happily.

The third section's epitaph reads, "Here lies a man who was right because he considered others right." These were people who were always happy because they had no complaints of others. Their happiness arose from a deep acceptance of life and others as they are.

While the third section sounds great, but it doesn't end here. There's a fourth section too.

The epitaph inscribed on these gravestones reads, "Here lies a body through which God expressed Himself."

A deeper look into the epitaph will reveal that it does not say, "Here lies a man…." The word "body" is used instead. This implies that in that body, the true Self was realized. The "body" abided in the Self and expressed the highest level of consciousness, leading an impersonal life (as opposed to an "individual" life). Those who gain true wisdom are the ones who are able to attain this state.

The first password helps you attain this true wisdom. Instead of being stuck in, "I am right" or "I don't care" or even "Everything is right in life and others are right," you progress to understanding who the "I" is. "Who am I?" helps you to understand yourself – your true nature. Instead of expecting people to understand you, it's far more vital to understand yourself. This means, you need to understand the first password, "Who am I?" in depth.

Thus, when you're faced with troubles, illness and suffering, it's essential to remind yourself, "I am a being full of love, joy, peace and vitality and I am currently passing through the tunnel of distress."

After some time, you'll see that the tunnel of distress has ended and you have arrived under the bright, open sky, leaving behind tunnels of all emotions.

Now, when you see a tunnel, smile at it. This is because now you have understood, **"Who I truly am is passing through the tunnels of distress, illness and troubles."** You'll always encounter all sorts of tunnels in your journey of life, but if you always remember your true identity, you'll always remain happy. Your way of looking at suffering will change.

Consider that you're driving your car and the fuel indicator signals the need to refuel. Does this make you unhappy? No. Instead. you happily fill it with petrol. You also understand and are thankful that your car is sending you this message. Why? Because it means your vehicle is working properly. Of course, if you ignore the many indications it's capable of giving you, your car will eventually break down.

Similarly, when you feel unhappy, remember who you truly are, recognize yourself and seek the truth. This is what refueling is. The truth is that your essence is happiness, and you're only passing through the small tunnel of unhappiness. If you remember this, you'll rejoice and sing joyfully even when you're in the middle of it and you're surrounded by nothing but darkness. If you can't do this, you'll keep singing the tunes of unhappiness that nobody understood you.

If it is clear to you that whatever you say and think, mother nature will strive to fulfill it as your command, you will be aware of your thoughts and careful with your speech. This is because you'd never want the negative thoughts and words to return to you multifold.

Therefore, instead of speaking negative, affirm and speak positive. If the first password is clear to you and you have understood it very well, then you will see that love, joy and peace will flourish in your life.

Whenever you see a tunnel labeled "suffering" or "unhappiness," know that it has arrived to remind you about your true joyful state that is beyond happiness and unhappiness. In short, whenever you feel unhappy, know that your true nature is joy.

Unhappiness is an indication – a feedback mechanism – by nature to remind you it's time to refuel and remind yourself of your true nature. If during this period, you find yourself unable to rejoice and sing joyfully, at least remind yourself, "I must not think negative now." Tell nature your side of the story, paint the true picture to the universe…

6

Tell Nature what you are in Favor of

How many times have you found yourself in this situation? You get angry over a situation or something someone said.

It's a natural reaction. Then you take this one step further. You get angry over the fact that you couldn't contain your emotions. So, now you're angry because . . . yes, because you got angry in the first place.

Sounds silly when it's stated like that, doesn't it? The fact of the matter is that you're not the only one who has ever reacted this way. Most people, when they discover this happening to them usually ask a question similar to this: "I can understand my initial reaction of anger. What I don't understand is why I get angry because I reacted that way."

Let's examine this to discover why you and many others find themselves in this predicament.

Let's assume, someone tells you, "Your child has failed his exams." As soon as you hear this, you disregard everything. Without even verifying the facts by checking his report card, you angrily lecture him about the importance of his trying his best and the importance of a good education. When your anger dies down slightly, you think about checking his report card. What you find shocks you. Your child didn't fail in his exams, he actually had excellent scores. A score so good, in fact, that he has actually scored very well and came in first in his class.

Now your anger turns into compassion and guilt. "I unnecessarily shouted at my adorable kid… He has actually scored more than what I had expected…. He quietly listened to my scolding without uttering a single word…" In this way, thoughts of guilt overwhelm your mind for a long time.

After feeling guilty, you once again feel angry, but this time, not at your child, but at your own foolishness. The next thing you know, you're mad at yourself because this isn't the first time you've reacted and got excited over a situation without a valid reason. This example illustrates what is meant by getting angry over your initial anger.

This is just a small example but there could be several such examples, where you tend to lose your cool. And once you get back to a balanced frame of mind, you get angry on your anger, "Why can't I exercise control over my anger?"

You can see why this happens. And you can understand why so many others, not just you, react like this. Once you calm down you're able to look at the situation from a different point of view.

The good news is that you're able to recognize that your initial reaction was unnecessary. The bad news is your reaction to it.

You must neither fight your anger and nor be angry at your anger.

It's not something that you don't already know. Most of us, at some point of our lives have experienced this "double anger." The reality of the situation is that the moment you experience emotion, your mind then states, "I'm very angry."

Remember those tunnels we passed through in the previous chapters of this book. That's exactly what's happening here. You're merely in the midst of the small tunnel of anger. The truth of the matter is that you're not the angry person. In reality, you're a loving person.

The moment you label yourself as angry, this erroneous statement is recorded in your brain and your future starts shaping to meet what you've declared.

The truth of the matter is that you are really "love." You're in favor of love and you have always been love. As you travel through this short tunnel, it's important to remember to ask these two questions: **"Who am I and who am I in favor of?"**

If you're not in favor of anger, tell yourself that immediately. Then follow that up with the positive affirmation: "I support love, joy and peace." This action which seems so slight a change of your thinking will actually make a world of difference in your outlook. It'll change your feeling. And you'll discover you won't need to be angry at your anger.

Whenever you are surrounded by disappointment and you can't shake it off, remind yourself, "I am a being filled with faith who is passing through the tunnel of disappointment; I am in favor of hope."

It's essential you clearly and unequivocally tell nature and yourself – what you do stand for. Remember that as soon as you specify it, nature immediately acts to fulfill it. As you begin to do this regularly, you'll be able to see a distinct change in your feelings. With your renewed feelings, you can then demand something new.

Be vigilant about your feelings

Always be vigilant about the feelings you hold for your intended aspirations. Take a pause occasionally to examine whether you have any unconscious negative feelings about the situation. Clear your feelings if there is any residual resistance.

For example, if you feel gripped with fear then re-affirm, "Though this feeling of fear is present, I am fully in favor of Faith and Courage." If you feel consumed by hatred, then re-affirm, "Though hatred is being felt, I am fully in favor of love and compassion."

Some negative feelings and their positive equivalents are given below:

Feeling	In favor of...
Anger	Love, Joy, Peace
Boredom	Enthusiasm
Comparison	Evenness
Depression	Bliss, Wonder, Joy
Ego	Witnessing Presence, Humility
Fear	Faith, Courage
Greed	Contentment
Hatred	Love, Compassion
Ill-will	Benevolence, Goodwill
Jealousy	Equanimity, Evenness

This is only a small sampling of how the cleansing of negative thoughts can be easily replaced by re-affirming their positive equivalents.

7

Stop Negative Affirmations

Many times, we think, "I don't like such a mother-in-law . . . I hope I don't get a husband like that . . . I hope my boss doesn't turn out to be a bad person." In this way, because of continuous use of words like "No", "Not" and "Don't", you'll continue to attract precisely the same people and situations which you don't approve of.

You must be clear what you want in your life, not what you don't. If you do this, the universe will provide you with synchronous surprises. You'll see the start of a beautiful relationship. The universe responds to your requests through the manifestation of all that you request, regardless of the item or the size.

As difficult as it may be to believe, the universe is fulfilling the prayers of everyone right now. That's the very reason why people come in contact with each other. The most magnificent and amazing thing about this simple fact is that it's occurring all the time. It's done without you having to do much more than to positively affirm it. It starts in motion a chain of events that you are totally unaware of. As soon as you do recognize that happening, the least you should do is to think positive thoughts.

When you believe yourself to be a limited body, you lead a confined life. You form wrong ideas about yourself. You go about your day freely thinking – and perhaps even affirming them out loud – such powerfully negative thoughts as "I am stupid, I am bad, I am unhappy, I am depressed…" What's even worse, you'll find yourself stuck in a rut. You can't get these concepts out of your head. After a while, you may even come to believe them. Many people do.

But, there's good news. Once you not only hold the password that opens all the locks, and you understand how you can use it, you can make equally powerful changes in your life. Once you reflect on it and practice using it, you'll free yourself from the bondage of these labels, mistaken identities and misconceived ideas.

You need to become firmly convinced that you aren't your body. You are, instead, eternally beyond that. It's then and only then, you'll be freed from all suffering.

This concept may be difficult for you to understand when it's first introduced. But what's your first thought when your shirt tears. Do you look at it and respond by saying, "I am torn?"

Of course not. Why? Because you're sure that you're not the shirt. The shirt is only something you wear to cover your body. In much the same way you're wearing your body, but you aren't the body. But our first thought, when the body falls ill, we say, "I am ill."

Because of this misconception, wrong results occur from your holding wrong beliefs. To overcome this, take the first steps in your action. That is to stop affirming negative sentences like, "I am poor, I am lazy, I am ill, I am in distress."

This won't happen overnight, but with even a bit of discipline and awareness, you'll discover not only how often you say statements like this, but how quickly you can change it around.

Otherwise, you'll discover yourself feeling overwhelmed by emotion. Irritation arises because of this. That leads to the committing of wrong actions and the indulgence of addictions. Many times, these overwhelmed individuals drink alcohol, pick fights with people and spoil their relationships. This goes to such an extent that husband and wife decide to separate because they can't control their painful emotions.

All because they don't understand what their emotions are trying to tell them. Most of the people haven't received the training to understand and decipher their emotions. At this point, it becomes difficult for them to control their emotions. Their thoughts, the emotions behind those thoughts, the suffering caused by these negative emotions, and their reactions to them – emotion, speech, thoughts, actions – together drag them farther and farther away from their goals.

Understanding the plan of action to use the first password and act on it, makes it possible for you to free yourself from all those thoughts causing you pain and suffering. Instead of training your brain to think and act out of hatred, anger, jealousy and sorrow, teach your mind about the thoughts of love, joy and peace. Teach yourself to be adept at handling your emotions. Then you can work past all of it and actually make progress, by forging ahead the ideas and concepts that have held you back. Your life will then be filled with prosperity, love, joy, energy, contentment and health.

8

The Second Password to a Happy Life

Every person you meet in your life plays a specific role, whether you realize it or not. Some individuals play a positive role; others play a negative one. When you spend time with those positive individuals, you'll know it. They inspire you to do more, to go farther to reach for your goals.

It seems obvious why your paths have crossed. They often show up at the right time in the right place. Or they're best friend and they always are there during what feels like the low moments of your life.

On the other hand, when you're around those individuals who play the negative roles, you'll feel as if life is nothing but a series of chores and drudgery. They bring your emotions down. Why? This occurs because when we're with them, we're not able to think beyond our own constrained methods of thinking.

If you think about it all, you may be asking yourself why you seem to run into these negative individuals. Sometimes you swear there's a long line of people auditioning for these negative roles – and they all seem to be competent at it.

Believe it or not, these people are just as vital in your life as the positive ones. They're in your life to bring your hidden dark areas into light. But, because you're unaware of this, as many people are, you get troubled by their presence. Instead of freeing yourself from that dark place, you chose, instead to lead a sorrowful life.

The second password: **Who is that?**

This, the second password to unlocking a happy life, refers to those individuals you meet along your journey. The first question you need to ask yourself is "Who is that?" Whoever he or she may be, you should be rest assured he had been placed there for a reason. He plays no minor role in your life. His true role, in fact, is to be a contributor in your life. He is your co-creator. This is true regardless of if they are negative or positive partners.

This, again, is not a concept that's easily grasped at first. Look at it like this:

If you wish to experience the ultimate heights of love, there'll be someone who'll make you feel hatred. But, you must not hate him. He, instead, deserves your compassion and mercy.

Imagine you want to play cricket and wish to bat first. You need a bowler for that. Unless someone does the bowling, you will not be able to bat. If there is no one to bowl, you will ask around, "Will you bowl for me?" Similarly, when a person desires, "Let me experience courage, let me pass through the tunnel of courage," someone arrives in his life to scare him. Only then he will be able to experience courage. The irony is that the other person is scaring you and at the same time bowling you, too.

Often, children play in a group. If a child doesn't have any friends and wishes to play cricket, he asks his father, "Will you play with me?" Since the father loves his son, he agrees to play with him. As the child prefers to bat, the father agrees to bowl him.

Then there is the game of chess. Undoubtedly you, under normal conditions need another person to play this game with you. You move your chess piece, then the other person moves his. The game continues like this. With every move, in fact, it becomes more interesting. If your competitor plays a smarter or a crooked move during his play, would you feel bad about it? No! It is because when your competitor plays different and new moves to defeat you, the game becomes all the more interesting. In fact, you find you're getting more interested in the game with each one of his moves.

Similarly, in the chess game of your life, when someone plays against you, defeats you every time, comes up with new moves, how do you react?

Do you worry and grow sad? If you do, then you have not understood the game at all. The reality is that the other person has arrived in your life to be a co-creator with you. He creates hurdles so that you're able to bring forth the dormant qualities lying within you. He'll help you express the goodness within you. If there is any such person in your life, he has come to enhance your life. Everything has been arranged for you in order to help you win this game of life.

If we carefully notice, each person has someone playing a negative role in his life. Sometimes there can be more than one people playing the role. As difficult as it might be to understand, those performing the negative role are doing so out of love for you. They too have forgotten this and you are unaware of this secret. This is exactly the purpose of the second password. It will remind you just this, "Who is that? Who is the other person?"

The father, out of love, will purposely throw a googly (akin to a curve ball in baseball) to his son so he can improve his skills. Let's say they're both unaware of the roles they're playing. If this is the case, the son becomes upset and unhappy with his father's action. He may think his father is treating him unfairly and groan, "Why does this always happen to me? When will I be happy? Where will I find love?" It wouldn't be surprising then he'll seek solution to his distress from someone other than his dad. Whether it's the father or the son, both must remember they have met each other for a specific purpose.

The husband and wife, too, are partners for each other in everything. All relationships, boss and employee, daughter-in-law and mother-in-law, all are nothing but partnerships. Someone wishes to bat, someone bowls to him or her. This is the law of life which forms the basis for relationships.

If you can't see, or refuse to see this, due to your limiting beliefs and short-sightedness, you continue to remain convinced that others are the cause of your distress. You'll be convinced, instead, that all these individuals are "out to get you" to ruin your life. You'll continue to ask, like the son who plays cricket with his father, "Why me?" These people are not in your life to "ruin you." This couldn't be farther from the truth, because whatever they do, they do it out of love. After all they are your partners.

In the next chapter, you'll learn the role your partner plays in your life.

9

Learn your Lessons from your Partner

With the first password you learnt to build a healthy relationship with your true Self. Now, using the second password let's learn how to build healthy relationships with others.

Whether you realize it or not, your relationships often turn sour because of your limiting beliefs and understanding. Therefore, it's important for you to firmly believe that the person who is playing a negative role in your life is a co-creator with you.

Whenever someone is consistently creating a stressful environment for you, ask yourself, "**Who is that?**" The answer is - he is your co-creator. He has something important which you must take from him. Yet, you're unable or refuse to learn what he's trying to teach. As long as you act this way, you'll find he continues to be the source of your stress and worry. If you want to break this cycle, then start accepting, even embracing, his efforts. Be open to receive that gift of teaching.

This is the secret. Once you decide to accept and apply it, you'll find the other person "changes." But that's not all, your "problem" also disappears seemingly all on its own.

Refuse to learn this and he'll continue to stress you out and provide plenty of negativity in your life. Whether you believe it or not, this is actually an arrangement made by nature for you. As soon as you become open to learning your lessons from him, accept him in your life, he will transform. That's it then! That was all the role that he was supposed to play in your life. Now, you will have a healthy relationship with him.

Your relationships with people remain tense until you accept them in your life for what they are – your co-creators. As long as you can't see them in this light or refuse to recognize the role they play for your benefit, you should expect nothing to change. This is the reason for their being in your life.

Look at it from this perspective. View him as a person who wants to give you a gift. He's sure it's something you've wanted all your life. But, you refuse to accept. Because he's so confident you'll love it, he stays with you until you finally take it from him.

Nothing changes until that moment when you accept his gift. It's as if magic occurs. The person transforms and your connection will automatically sweeten with him. This is why you must learn your lessons as soon as you can. This puts you at ease with this individual. But more than that, you'll also have helped him in accomplishing his own goal, his mission in life. In this way, both of you will succeed in completing your goals.

Knowing what you know now, carefully review your life. You'll see that there have been many people coming in and out of your life. When you first met some of these individuals, you were sure there was no way you'd get along with them. Your relationships with them were strained at first. But as you "got to know them" as we so often say, the relationship improved.

If, however, if you're still discovering hurdles, trying to block your way, there's some rejection involved and the reason is you. The second password then – the question of **"Who is the other person?"** – will remind you of these past relationships. And because of that, you'll get an insight and nearly immediately say, "The other person has brought out his worst to bring out the best in me."

When you get exasperated with your interaction with him, you just might announce, "Now, it's enough! It is too much… I will not leave him… I'll do this… I'll say this…"

In any tense incident, ask yourself, "Who is he?" The answer is - the other person is your co-creator and the incident has presented himself as an opportunity to enhance your abilities. If the other person has played his moves, has played his cards, you will play your cards of love, joy and peace.

The other person has become a villain to make you a superstar.

He's playing the bad guy to help you bring your good side to the surface. With this understanding, you'll develop gratitude towards the other person for his part. Otherwise, you'll remain unaware of the true reason these individuals have arrived in your life.

The true reason is to provide you with an opportunity to help you express your divine qualities. Remember that when the valleys are deeper, the mountains also attain greater heights.

Imagine what the writing on a normal black chalkboard looks like. The white chalk is crisp, easy to read, and is bright compared to the black background. This is because the black of the board enhances and brings out the clarity of the white writing. The presence of evil is an opportunity for the divinity to surface. In the same way, darkness brings out the light; falsehoods and deceit become an opportunity to reveal the truth.

In the play of cricket, **if a player repeatedly bowls a bouncer, it presents an opportunity for the batsman to hit a sixer.** In the same way, life throws a bouncer at you through negative situations. You must hit a sixer by giving the right response to the bouncer; that is boost your qualities.

A cricketer who wishes to be an expert in his play will not be afraid of incoming bouncers. Despite sustained injuries on the field, sledging from the opposite team players, he remains focused on any opportunity that will let him play a four or a sixer. He is eager and ready to perform his best during the play. Likewise, you must be ready to enhance the divine qualities within you.

10

Safeguard your Diamonds

Whenever an unhappy event occurs in your life or someone creates hurdles, it's only human nature to eventually complain, "This person always does this… Because of him my life has become hell… He is purposefully creating obstacles for me…"

You know now, though, that these words are nothing more than a form of negative thinking. Change your perspective, see him as a gift of the universe and learn your lesson from him. Tell yourself that's what happening right now, however, unpleasant, is actually occurring to groom you.

Life is a game of snakes and ladders. The one who becomes an expert in playing the game, does not fear losing. We face several snakes in the form of difficulties and problems in our lives as well. Anyone can climb a ladder, but **a person who can use a snake as a ladder and progress further is truly known as a successful person, a winner.**

A winner never loses focus of his goal. Howsoever many difficulties he may need to encounter, he never complains, nor blames, but keeps his focus only on his ultimate success. He keeps progressing. He reaches his goal, crossing all the hurdles. Otherwise, some people are stuck only in complaints and blames.

You would obviously have noticed such people. Their mornings begin with a complaint, "I slept less today." The first word that they use is "less." These people always find that they have less of everything in their life. They never say, "I have more than enough, I have too much, I have abundance." They never make use of such words.

People who complain, start their day with statements like, "Today I slept little. I got less time to complete work... The maid worked less today... The milkman gave less milk today... The power went midway and that's why I had less of warm water for use today... The neighbor dumped his garbage in front of my home..." Such a person complains from morning to night, whether about the office, shop, school, college or something else. Apart from being with a negative attitude, they always find faults in others. They blame others for their mistakes and hold other people accountable for their problems.

Due to their negative thoughts, they attract similar situations in their lives. Hence, instead of using the word "less" you must affirm to nature, "I have everything in abundance. I am in favor of abundance. The sleep that I received was enough." This is because the body's needs undergo a change every day. Sometimes the body needs more sleep and sometimes less, and how much ever it gets, it is enough.

Once you know this secret and actively use it in your life, surprising changes will begin to happen. Love, joy and peace will begin to grow. Choose to try it. Once you take one day – just one day – living in this way, you'll begin to realize that you can actually live the rest of your life in this manner. If you don't muse out loud, you'll at least think the following: "I never knew that a life could be lived like this. Now that I know this is how I am going to live. The understanding I now have is as precious like a diamond that I will treasure."

Those who own diamonds, know their worth and are extremely vigilant about safeguarding them and keeping a watchman. A beggar will never hire a watchman. Only those who have diamonds will be aware and can say, "I will never let anyone rob me of my diamonds of love, joy, peace, happiness, satisfaction, health, and vigor. I will appoint the watchman of awareness. I will always maintain this awareness because I am in favor of love, joy, peace, happiness, satisfaction, health, and vigor." When you affirm this repeatedly, it will reach your subconscious mind and you will be able to live complaint-free.

In chapter 8, we looked at one possible answer when we applied the second password. by asking who is that? The other person is a co-creator, a partner.

The other person has arrived to help me win in the game of life by helping me to remember to safeguard my diamonds (states) of love, joy and peace.

In chapter 9, you became aware of another answer. The other person is someone who has arrived to bring out the best in you. Use any of these answers to apply the second password to transcend any complaints you may have or unhappiness you may have with others.

11

The Third Password to a Happy Life

Life's short and fleeting. Your life – and everyone else's – is but a speck on the universal timeline. We've been told this before and undoubtedly will hear it again. Most of us, though, are so taken with our own lives, so captivated by the world around us that we become nearly oblivious to everything else. Our lives become our first priority. Because of that we don't give the expanse of time much thought.

But honestly, there's another reason we tend to disregard these words. The programming of our mind through our genes and our particular upbringing make us experience this world in certain fixed ways. In effect, this method of thinking has made us prisoners to the small concepts and ideas. The majority of us, at least for some period of our lives, have believed this without even questioning the validity of these views.

Because of this, your life, if you review it closely has been based on two broad goals. The first is to chase after pleasant and enjoyable experiences or you've spent your time in an attempt to avoid unpleasant ones.

But, how do you decide what's pleasant or unpleasant? Let's look at the habit of cigarette smoking. You may find it unpleasant, even repugnant. Your neighbor, though, enjoys smoking. Why do the two of you view the same experience from different perspectives?

The truth of the matter is that the nature of the world is neither pleasant nor unpleasant. It is what it is – without labels, without bias. The nature of the world depends on how you relate to it. Your past and how you reacted to it and currently view it are an important indication on how you're going to view the present moment, as well as how you predict what the future holds for you.

But, these aren't the criteria you base your views of the world. You – and in fact all of us – then label what we see and experience – be it people or objects, situations or experiences. The moment you label something, you in effect "cover it up." You stop seeing the truth of it. Its essence is lost to you.

Your world is a screen upon which you project your own mental traits, your unresolved emotions, your strengths and deficiencies. What you view as the world is, in reality, a reflection of what you project.

It's intriguing that different people react to the same events in vastly different ways. Why does this happen? It's because incidents have no meaning by themselves, unless meanings are superimposed through thoughts. And the same incident can cause entirely different thoughts in different people.

This is because they're projecting or superimposing their own mental baggage on the screen, then watching the scene through their own mental filters. When they do this, it distorts the picture of reality.

This leads us to the ultimate reality that there is no absolute world out there! That may seem incredible. Many individuals, when they first hear this, refuse to believe it. The truth of the matter is that you're constantly shaping your own personalized world as you go through life. Everything you experience, including people and situations are shaded by your perceptions and are projections of what is held deep within your mind. More often than not, you're lost in the external details to such an extent that you don't realize that these details are only living pictures of what lies buried within your mind.

No situation is good or bad. No incident or situation is inherently a problem in and of itself. A situation is a situation, nothing more, nothing less. It becomes a so-called problem, triggers blame or you view it negatively only because you're viewing it through the filters of your limiting beliefs.

The experiences that we go through in life are like mirages in a desert. A mirage is an image many individuals, as they travel through a hot desert that's been created by their brain. They are convinced of the reality of the image right until the moment they walk up to it and it disappears.

What you see and label as the "world" around you isn't actually what is there. We don't see things for what they truly are. Once we're aware of this and see through the mirage, then we need to break through the very cause why the mirage appears to exist. And the root cause is the judgmental and comparing faculty of the mind that creates worrying and frightening apparitions. This faculty of the mind needs to be brought down.

How can you avoid being trapped by the conditioning of your mind?

It's actually much simpler than most individuals suppose it to be. You learn the art of asking yourself the right questions in various life situations – questions that will lead you from what seems to be obvious on the surface to the deeper transcendental truth. Such questioning can break through the illusions that appear in various circumstances, so that you can smile when faced with any illusion, without getting deluded.

If you don't ask the mind the proper question, then it will just continue to allow you see the situation as the illusion painted by its underlying beliefs. And this will continue to allow you to complain and grumble, "Life is difficult; people don't cooperate; my children will abandon me; old age is setting in."

It's impossible to experience peace of mind when you're continually plagued by thoughts like these? The secret from your being released from the images is simple but it may demand a bit of discipline on your part to achieve.

You need to learn the art of asking the right questions and apply it whenever you are caught up in such an illusory maze. When you ask yourself the right questions at the right time, it reminds you to shift your perspective from what you believe you see to its deeper truth.

The Third Password

The third password to a happy life is a question that can break through the illusory maze of beliefs and assumptions and throw light on the reality of the situation. The question is: **"Is this an illusion, a fact, a truth or the divine truth?"** When you ask yourself this question, it can free you from the unhappiness that you experience in various situations.

This is the only way to look past your assumptions, deep-seated notions and limiting beliefs of your mind. As soon as you transcend these assumptions, you will begin to feel a natural state of peace.

What is an illusion, a fact, a truth and the divine truth?

To apply this question and break through the illusion of everyday situations, you first must understand what is meant by each of these terms.

Illusions

An illusion implies a misconception. Something seems to be true but it's not. You've heard of optical illusions. You swear that you see what you think, but when you look at it from a different angle, it's something completely different.

For example, when a long stick is dipped halfway in water, it looks as if it's bent at the point where it is dipped. But we know that it's not really bent. In the dark, a rope may appear like a snake. A coat hanging in the dark may appear like a ghost.

These are obvious illusions of the material world, which have no bearing on our happiness. The illusions, though, that arise due to your misconstrued assumptions and limiting beliefs will continue to lead you to see your relationships, your life situations and incidents in ways that torment you, causing depression and bitterness. It's this, second, subtler illusion that we need to scrutinize through conscious questioning.

Consider the example of wealth. If your thoughts are impoverished, insatiable and complaining, then even though you amass a lot of money, you will only buy a hell for yourself. You'll find yourself begging for more, albeit with a golden bowl. Without an understanding of the truth of life, even being wealthy is a curse. There are many rich people who are victims of stress, depression and disease. So, money, in and of itself, isn't the password to a happy life.

But there are people who keep blaming their unhappiness on their lack of money. When you think this way, you need to stop, survey the situation and ask yourself this question: "Is this an illusion? Is it my myth that rich people are always happy? Aren't there people who are wealthier than me and yet dissatisfied?" When you do this, your mind gains clarity that your view is nothing more than an illusion. By asking this question you have the opportunity to break through past the illusion and finally come to a sense of peace.

Facts and Truths

Let's now consider the difference between facts and truth. You believe what you're thinking is a fact. But how can you be sure. One quick way to tell is to know you have logic and experience to prove facts. That being said, we're going to muddy the waters a bit here and add that not every fact is necessarily the truth.

Sounds absurd? Imagine this situation then.

At night, it's a fact that the sun has set. However, the truth is that the sun neither sets nor rises; it stays fixed relative to the Earth. It's the position of the Earth that changes as it rotates. So that statement you hold as fact is, indeed, a fact, but not precisely the truth.

Even the moon changes its shape every day. This is a fact. Sometimes it's a half moon and sometimes full moon. But, the truth is that it remains as it is; it neither waxes nor wanes. The Earth's shadow cast on the moon is what makes it appear to be changing shape throughout the month.

Here's an illustration that you'll answer with such certainty, that you'll find yourself scratching your head when you realize the "truth."

Is the water in this glass cold, or is it warm? The answer lies in relativity. If your left hand is cold, then the warm water may feel hot. If your right hand is hot, then the warm water may feel relatively cool. It then turns out that your left hand does not agree with your right hand over something so simple and obvious as the temperature of water. So, does this mean your own body is lying to you!? Both the hands are stating their facts, but none of them is telling the truth. The truth is that the water is neither hot nor cold.

Consider the case of wealth again. It could be a fact that one is not financially well off. But then, "Is it the truth?" The truth about wealth is that every scene is a preparation for the next future scene. You create your future by the seeds of feelings that you plant in the present. When you are gripped by feelings of despair and scarcity, you plant seeds of a future that you don't actually desire.

However, when you have faith in this law of nature, you'll change your feelings and honor abundance with faith. If you can dwell in joy and faith, regardless of the situation-at-hand, then you're truly wealthy! This uncompromising joy makes you a magnet that attracts the best things in your life.

Divine truth

And now we come to the final question.

"What is the divine truth… the ultimate truth… the absolute reality?"

When you ask yourself this question, you're reminded of the ultimate truth that everything that's happening is only a vehicle for the real Self to experience its nature and express its divine qualities. Self is enacting through different body-minds and carrying forward its game in this world. When you can see this, you then shift from the limited personal standpoint to the universal standpoint of the Self.

Asking this question awakens you, it challenges your beliefs and throws light on the darkness that up until this point seemed to engulf you.

The purpose of this questioning is to develop unshakeable clarity so you can be in bliss, regardless of innumerable ominous problems that seem to loom over you. It's to gain the maturity that the tides may continue to rise and fall, but you remain untouched, unsullied and carefree forever.

And arriving at this place in life really is simple. It's all about asking the right question at the right time. People tend to ask the wrong questions, which lead them into further quandary. Or else, they tend to ask the right questions at the wrong time.

Every decision you take, every choice you make, conveys whether you are trapped in the illusion of your mental world or in clarity and conviction of your true nature. The thoughts you entertain in testing situations ultimately are the cause of what "shakes you up." Thoughts that are impoverished and injured can cause you to see darkness in bright daylight.

Whenever you encounter a thought that saddens you, become alert and make use of the third password. Immediately ask yourself, "Is this an illusion? Does this thought hold so much power that it can upset me? What are the facts behind this thought that are making me grieve? Is it the truth? What is the divine truth? When you ask the right questions, you'll be able to see the truth. For example: "What is suffering? Why do we suffer? Where does it really arise?"

For example, suppose that thoughts similar to the following pop into your head: "Will I be cheated? Will someone swindle me? Will the bankers commit any blunder? There is so much fraud happening these days…" When this happens, your first and most essential step is to calm yourself.

Then ask yourself, "Are these thoughts based on an illusion, a fact, or the truth? What is the divine truth?" By using the right line of questioning you can contemplate and even overcome your negative self-talk: "Maybe this could be my illusion. I need not worry until I visit the bank and find the truth. Mere worrying will not give me any solution. I will be cautious of my future transactions…" In this way, you can keep yourself away from the trouble caused by your thoughts.

Let's understand the details of this password in the next chapter and see how we can apply it in our lives to lead a life free from suffering.

12

The Truth Hides behind your Illusion

Certain situations and events in life can cause us to be deluded. It means that there's a gap between what the mind believes and the actual truth of the situation.

So, in keeping with your preconceived ideas and limiting beliefs your mind laments and swiftly moves to several thoughts that sound a lot like those below, in all probability.

"The world is going through a period of recession. Will I lose my job? Will my business lose its market share? Will I be able to sustain my financial inflow? I'm getting older and before I know I'll face old age and illness… These days, even kids do not come to help…. How can I cope with the inflated cost of living? The weather is worsening. Every year, it's becoming hotter during summers, colder during winters and rains are scanty; how will we as a society survive? Cancer has now become such a common ailment; hope I don't get inflicted by it…"

There's no end to the constant chatter of the deluded mind.

How could anyone hope to remain peaceful in the midst of a storm of thoughts like these?

Being entangled in such a web of imagined thoughts, many people sleepwalk through their lives.

An individual who can't stop his talkative and judgmental mind with the right questions will lead a life of stupor and apathy. That's why when you feel worried, you must question each of your thoughts. You should be asking yourself: "Whatever I'm seeing is causing me suffering, insecurity, and depression. Is this the truth or merely an illusion of my mind?"

As discussed in the previous chapter you need to shoot the arrow of right questions at the judgmental mind. That's the only way to get to the cause of the illusion and unravel the truth.

"Is this an illusion, a fact, the truth or the divine truth?" With this question, hidden aspects will emerge. When the truth begins to shine forth through the illusion, you'll feel tranquil.

For example, imagine you're waiting for your medical diagnostic reports. You have a flurry of thoughts bouncing around your mind, that sound like something like this. "I don't know how the tests will turn out. I hope it's not this illness." In this situation, ask, "Is this an illusion, a fact, the truth or the divine truth?"

Your first step is to calm your mind. No, you don't know the results yet, but approach that with a calmness and tranquility. Why should you get upset and fearful when you don't have any idea what the diagnosis is? Then, regardless of the outcome of the tests your thoughts are healthy and beautiful, and no report can cause you suffering.

Let's understand how this password can be practically applied by reviewing what can be done in several instances.

Is it really cold today?

There are times when the weather feels severe to many of us. Come winter and it's common to hear remarks like this: "It's really cold today." There are also some who have associated some fixed feelings with weather conditions. Winter can be depressing for some, while the sweating summer days can bring irritation and anger within others.

The third password can be helpful in bringing these programmed reactions to the weather to light. First, you'll ask yourself, "Is this an illusion?" You may retort, "But if I am feeling cold, it's unquestionable. How can it be an illusion!" Then prod yourself further by asking, "Is this a fact?"

You might answer, "It's obvious. See, I'm wearing a sweater." But then, "Is this the truth?" You may reply, "How can it not be true? When it's biting cold, how can I ignore it?"

However, the truth is that "cold temperature" or "hot weather" are not empirical truths. It is relative to what one is used to as a part of one's upbringing. Someone who is brought up in a tropical weather can feel cold even when the temperature drops to 15 degrees Celsius. On the other hand, someone who is used to living in temperate or polar conditions may find 15 degrees warm and pleasant.

The truth is that people associate facts with how they are feeling within. If the weather feels cold today, it could be because your body is feeling dull and sluggish. Cold is felt depending on the condition of your body.

This might not make much sense when you first read it but give it some thought. When you're assigned a boring job, then seconds working on it can feel agonizingly long. If you're working on something you love you start the project and poke your head out of work hours later, wondering where the time went.

Similarly, if you're watching one of your favorite movies, the potentially long length of the film flies by. What does this illustrate? These are all excellent illustrations that the terms "less time" or "more time" are really both illusions. The truth is that there is neither less nor more time. Time only is.

Does the other person really hate me?

Similarly, you can become a victim of your illusions even with regard of the relationships you experience. When people behave in undesirable, unpleasant or unexpected ways, you naturally tend to jump to thoughts like: "He hates me… He doesn't care for me… He's a bad person." The next time you begin to think this way, consider that what you've heard or experienced is an illusion and not the truth at all.

And in fact, the thoughts you entertain regarding the other person are actually an illusion. The truth is that we mold the personalities of those around us based on our own beliefs and assumptions. When we do, then we see individuals in that way, our beliefs are only getting reinforced or validated. When that happens you may even say, "See… I knew that he's such a person. I am not surprised that he behaved this way."

Your illusions you hold about others won't break – can't break – until you begin to reconcile and clarify them. You do this by asking the proper question. And that question is "What does the fact indicate?

How true is this? Or is this the divine truth?" You will get your answer.

Are people really bad?

Even just your thoughts that "People are bad" can be an open invitation to allow "bad" people into your life. Your thoughts, you'll remember create your reality. Though it may seem unbelievable, you actually attract situations and people into your daily life according to the beliefs and assumptions that you harbor within the mind.

Is this an illusion, then?

Yes, when you approach people from this perspective, you're absolutely looking at this individual's behavior and words as illusion. And you can point to supporting facts for this. But the truth of the matter is that people are not bad. They are, in all reality, bound by their own tendencies. And these tendencies force them to helplessly behave and speak in ways that you consider are bad.

When you feel negative feelings arise you may not even be aware of what is occurring. You know people, without a doubt, individuals who shout angrily and blame those around them for situations they find themselves in.

Let's face it, at one time or another everyone needs to vent their emotions. You only have to look around and see examples around us on a daily basis. Parents talk angrily with their children, managers shout at their employees. These both are good examples of the venting process.

Consider a child who returns home from school, throws his bag, shoes and water bottle around the house as he flies through the house, stomping his feet in anger.

Is he a bad person? Not necessarily. It's entirely possible that one of his teachers reprimanded him. He may have been involved in an argument with close friends. When his mom sees him act this way, she doesn't think of him as a bad child. In fact, she treats his behavior as an illusion.

Mom understands that something may have caused this extraordinary behavior due to something that upset him. Because of this, she realizes the best way to handle him is to allow him to release his stress through this way, even if it means to allow him to grumble for a while.

When parents consciously love their children, the children at some point then let go of their negative and disruptive behavior. But, parents should know how to handle these situations, instead of venting their feelings through negative thoughts and words. Their responses, though, is not entirely their fault. They are unaware that the child's bad behavior is merely an illusion combined with their own stressors.

With the above example in mind, consider the following scenario. A good friend, who you've known for years is filled with anger and said, "Don't talk to me ever again!" What should you do? You should ignore his words. That's right. Instead you need to patiently and intently listen to what he's saying with empathy, even if your friend is shouting.

Allow him to vent. Once he has the venting out of his system, it's not out of the question that he'll return and thank you. He'll express his appreciation that you allowed him the freedom to do that.

That seemingly amazing transformation in his behavior only

occurred because you know your friend inside out. You know what is "true" about him. You're aware that he's helpless at times due to his tendencies. And these tendencies trigger strong emotions within him. The result? He gets angry.

So, the fact that "people are bad" is not really a fact at all. Now you can see the truth that hides behinds the facts. The truth, instead, reveals that "people aren't bad. They are, however, helpless. Their own deep-seated tendencies are the reasons they behave in ways which you would think they were bad."

What they need at this point is your help in releasing their negative emotions. You can do this simply by listening to them. This, in many ways, is the single most important thing you can do for them.

Evil is indirectly supporting goodness

For some, this may be difficult to understand. The presence of evil is indirectly supporting goodness. But, think about it. It's because of the evil in this world, in whatever form, that goodness is actually valued. Because of evil, you're able to see the important role the good plays in this world. It's because of evil that you actually value goodness.

Let's look at it this way, you value honesty, because of all the dishonesty you see around you. If there were nothing labeled "bad" then there would be nothing labeled "good." This is the divine truth.

If evil is helping the value of goodness, then how could it possibly be bad? Evil, so it seems, turns out to be indirectly good. Stains, for example, are good. They serve as the cause for cleansing.

In this way, perhaps you can now see the goodness that rests in supposedly bad individuals. If you can see it this way, then your own outlook toward these individuals will shift. The thoughts of hatred or disdain you have for them will vanish.

Some examples were given in this chapter. Now, you need to investigate the illusory truths of your life; verify them with the help of the third password. You will then be able to validate their reality. Let's understand more about it in the next chapter.

13

Two Principles of Life – Illusion and the Bright Truth

Every day, you look at the illusion and believe it to be the truth.

Let's look at the businessman who suddenly had a thought rush through his head: "My business is affected by the recession we're in."

It seems like a natural enough thought, there again. What if the thought were only an illusion? Others though don't think that. They actually feel the evidence of it and see the proof of recessions at every turn.

What do they see? They see a downturn in business, less sales than a year ago at this time. And because of this, they treat this so-called evidence as accepting the fact that a recession exists.

What is the truth?

The truth is the recession is, in reality, preparation for a new beginning. That's right. Whenever a recession occurs, the world actually has reached newer and greater heights.

The divine truth hidden behind this is that nature interrupts the workings of the world by pausing events for a moment. Some events occur to stimulate that recession. What happens then. People are forced to think creatively in order to overcome the recession. These individuals take the positive initiative and new solutions to old problems are found, new ideas get created. And because of all of this, higher, brighter summits are reached. This is the way the world works toward making progress.

Consider that a store owner sometimes thinks, "I should be able to have a monopoly in and around my area. Then, everyone would have come to my store to buy anything." In a similar vein, when others think about the possibility of establishing a monopoly in their segment of industry, the economy sometimes tumbles out of balance. These types of thoughts only manifest into a reality on a larger scale, which in turn causes nature to interfere to change the system.

Nature desires newer inventions at some point of time. That means people must rethink their actions. They need to be flexible in order to conduct themselves with a newer thought process for these new times. They need to abandon their age-old ways of working and embrace the new.

When you're not able to learn something new, a recession of sorts emerges in your life, forcing you to think. This doesn't mean nature hates you. Whatever incidents are taking place on earth are here for one purpose, to awaken you from your slumber. This is nature's love for you.

Whenever you're faced with change, you now know that it's appearing in your life to lift you out of your old pattern of thinking. Once you can understand this as the divine truth, then you can pass through this period of your life without putting up any resistance. You need to remember to ask the proper questions and then think about the answers seriously. It may even mean you need to increase the length of your contemplation and meditation sessions to truly understand the divine truth hidden behind the illusions of your changes. In this way, you'll free yourself from the flood of illusory thoughts and alleviate the unnecessary suffering that it brings.

Below are a few examples which illustrate some sample illusions people commonly face and are troubled with. You need to find the divine truth hidden behind them and focus your attention on it.

Fact	:	I'm the person who has to clean the house every day.
Illusion	:	It's untidy and dirty everywhere.
Truth	:	I'm living this life to cleanse myself from within. This means removing negativity from my mind.
Divine Truth	:	While purifying myself within, I want to instill devotion in me.

◆ ◆ ◆

Fact	:	He turned away the moment he saw me.
Illusion	:	Typically, I'm not an angry person by nature. People deliberately force me to act that way
Truth	:	People are helping me in enhancing my patience and fortitude by nudging me to contemplate on my anger.
Divine Truth	:	God is playing various roles with me through various people out of love to enhance the divine qualities within me.

Fact	:	I am stranded in the office to complete my tasks; no one invites me to their parties.
Illusion	:	I am sad and lonely.
Truth	:	I am getting the opportunity to meditate on this feeling of sadness; I am realizing that I am not lonely, but alone (all-one).
Divine Truth	:	The truth is that I am the blissful sense of Beingness, which is the same in one and all.

◆ ◆ ◆

Fact	:	I was fired from my job.
Illusion	:	I am a failure. I am a misfit.
Truth	:	This is an opportunity to learn the vital lessons of patience and perseverance.
Divine Truth	:	Every scene is a preparation for the next scene according to my divine plan.

◆ ◆ ◆

Fact	:	My associate cheated me.
Illusion	:	People always tend to trouble me.
Truth	:	This is an opportunity to strengthen my resolve to be upright and compassionate.
Divine Truth	:	I want to express the qualities of God because I am a part of Him. My body is just a medium for divine expression.

Fact	: My house has been robbed
Illusion	: The world is a bad place. People are dishonest and can't be trusted.
Truth	: It's time to awaken the wellspring of unfaltering faith within me.
Divine Truth	: Realize the untouched immaculate Self that you truly are by removing all doubts.

◆ ◆ ◆

Fact	: I have pain in my knees.
Illusion	: I am unwell. I am weak.
Truth	: Pain is my body's feedback.
Divine Truth	: The Real 'I' is far, far away from illness. No illness can touch me.

We understood how the third password can be used in different situations to investigate and verify the illusory truths of our lives. We can then discern how our perceptions can be either illusions or facts and decipher the truth or the divine truth behind them.

14

The Fourth Password to a Happy Life

It goes without saying that in today's competitive world, almost everyone lives a stressful life.

Even the smallest of problems make us unhappy. Not only that, but for the most part you then feel it's only logical to experience that unhappiness when faced with problems.

You feel that you are always gripped by some problem or the other which seems to lead to one long sorrowful life. You find it impossible to be happy in all situations. You make it clear that whether in the office or at home or in one of your relationships, there exists negative situations that trigger unhappiness. You wonder, "How can I stay happy in all situations? It's easier said than done."

If you wish to be happy in all situations, you can do so by all means because happiness is your essential nature. Everybody wants to be happy at all times, in all situations. But when you find yourself getting stuck in certain situations, you also discover that you're not happy.

There's a simple, single phrase that plays a vital role in helping to retain the happiness in your life, if you'd only allow it, regardless of the circumstances you find yourself in. In fact, you can use it by its simple acronym: IDM.

Before you go thinking it means something about an antiballistic missile, **IDM stands for "It Doesn't Matter."** That's right. This is the fourth password to unlocking a happy life.

You may dismiss them as three trivial words, but you'd be dismissing one of the valuable passwords that can lead you to happiness.

When used with the proper understanding they can prove to be most powerful. By using this password, you'll be able to accept every negative circumstance without suffering. Thus, whenever you accept any negative situation, it means you have made use of the IDM password.

Let's understand how this password can be used in your day-to-day life through an example.

When someone ridicules you, you feel bad. But the moment you say, "It Doesn't Matter," you'll stop feeling bad about it or at the very least, you'll feel some relief. Not only that, but the larger picture is that you'll be able to accept his behavior.

Whenever you don't like someone's response, you naturally grumble, "Why didn't he respond properly? Why does he always have to act that way? I'll get him back and he better watch out."

However, the moment you say, "It Doesn't Matter," you'll gain a new perspective. You become open to accept the other person's behavior and your mind becomes clear.

When we resist a situation, it's like building banks along the river of unhappiness. This in turn deepens the river. When we accept our suffering with the IDM password, it's like placing the situation in the magic box of acceptance. When the banks of resistance are removed, the river of unhappiness dissolves in the ocean of acceptance.

Understand it this way; whenever we refuse to accept the suffering in any situation, we create a bank for it. Thus, leading to accumulation of more suffering. And when we accept the suffering by saying, "It Doesn't Matter," we do not let a bank build up, thus letting the suffering wash away.

There's only one way you can create a solution to a problem. And that's to place it in the magic box of acceptance.

Many of the greatest scientists and inventors have used this method, whether they realized it or not. They're in the middle of trying to solve a stubborn problem but keep coming up empty-handed. So, they placed the problem in that magic box of acceptance. Before they realized it, while their mind was unoccupied, they would suddenly find a solution. Many times, the solution would come to them in the shower or while bathing.

You may wonder why does it happen. To continue with our magic box metaphor, the moment you place the item in the box, it begins to change. Your mind, whether you realize it or not, then recites the password IDM.

Between these two events, a new way of solving the problem begins to emerge. Your mind still works on the problem, but now it does so in the background. The moment you resist that problem, your mind shuts down, it simply refuses to work on it.

The beauty of the IDM password is that you'll avoid that whole "getting upset" over it stage. You'll no longer be bogged down by the trivial matters of your day-to-day living.

The IDM password is an even more valuable tool should you ever be hit with a major crisis. The key to making it work though is to accept the situation while trying to find solutions to the problem.

With the aid of this password, you'll be able to keep your stable state of mind. Your mind will "melt away" any and all resistance that occurred because of another person's negative behavior. And in that state, it will be free from the suffering and start looking at a solution immediately.

Now, when anyone should ask about that problem, you can say, "It's in the magic box of acceptance waiting to be resolved."

This is easy enough to do with smaller problems. It's not that hard to take the smaller jabs of life, place them in the magic box and then accept them. If you try this with the larger obstacles of life and succeed to some degree, it means that you have achieved the ability to use this password in all situations.

When you use this in some circumstances, be prepared to take some heat from others. For example, let's say a member of your family isn't feeling well. Others in your family are worried and unhappy about his illness. They wish he would get well as quickly as possible. When you use the IDM password here, prepare yourself for a backlash. Your reaction will be something along the following description:

You know that his illness doesn't affect you negatively, so you appear not to be sympathizing in the manner that other family members are. They immediately conclude that you don't care. They conclude you don't love him. But the larger question is - can love be expressed only through a grieving process.

As a matter of fact, that's what many people believe. If you don't react the same way as they do, then you obviously aren't compassionate. In fact, some of your family members may even believe that you lack love. It's certainly a sign that you aren't sympathetic. Obviously, these individuals believe that the only way to react to someone else's suffering is by suffering alongside him.

They believe they're suffering for the welfare of the one who is feeling ill. Even the person who's ill finds solace and believes that others are suffering with them out of love. Let's understand this example a bit farther.

Why do others suffer because a family member has fallen ill? They believe this action is in the best welfare of the person who's ill. But, while the ill person finds this comforting, there's one big problem with this. The ill person already has a low state of consciousness. He's already in a negativity. Then he finds himself interacting with family members who are also suffering because of the situation. The final result? The ill individual will only experience more suffering. Your sympathy, expressed in this manner, hasn't done any good. It may, have in fact only made things worse.

The saddest part of this story is that the ill person and other family members don't realize what's happening. If they grieve in the other person's suffering, it's because of their attachment and blind love for the other. Some people call this simply ignorance and superstition.

Are you serious in helping the ill family member get over his medical problems? The best way to do this is listen to him but remain happy. Yes, you read that properly. Remain happy.

The other person, at this moment in time, is unable to stay happy for any length of time. Chances are good that he'll appreciate your upbeat attitude. Your higher level of consciousness and positive vibrations will help him come out of his suffering.

When you make use of the IDM password even in big situations, you'll notice that those situations no longer affect you. In this way, you'll remain happy even in negative situations.

15

The Fifth Password to a Happy Life

Perhaps one of the biggest advantages of a positive outlook is that you have lessened your pain and your negativity in these situations.

Of course, your suffering won't disappear overnight. Instead, the pain and negativity will diminish gradually. And it's not eliminated permanently. You'll still be facing with feelings of sadness every now and then.

The question then becomes, "What is the permanent solution for freedom from suffering?"

Whenever you feel unhappy or gloomy in any situation, you need to look within yourself. You'll discover an underlying erroneous root belief or fallacious story that is triggering this.

Don't keep this story inside of you. Instead, remove it from the protection of darkness within you and allow it to hit the light of day. This is the lasting solution for the liberation from what the world calls suffering.

Once you begin to get into the habit of looking within yourself, you allow reality to enter into your life. You're able to harmonize with reality. You'll love and accept everything that enters your life. And you'll be able to accept all events, both good and bad with a view that "it is as it is" without grumbling over them.

You'll certainly find faults in others and then become disappointed or feel hurt. However, **the fault lies in your thought, "There is fault in others," and this thought lies within you. Therefore, you need to stop finding fault in others and cleanse yourself from within.**

This is the fifth password to a happy life. When you use this password and make it a part of your life, then you'll realize that instead of blaming the other, you need to work upon yourself.

The way to apply this password is that whatever fault you see in others, notice that the same may be the case with you and cleanse yourself by repeating an affirmation that affirms the opposite.

Here's a situation you've probably been in before. Something has gone wrong in your workplace. Your colleagues as well as your supervisor blame for the misunderstanding. You know beyond a shadow of a doubt it wasn't your fault.

Instead of immediately sinking into negative thoughts, or pointing your finger at someone else, blaming him, affirm this: "I am surrounded by love and truth."

Understand that since blame is within you, this complaint about others has manifested on the outside. Basically, the world is a mirror. You should be focusing on the goodness you want to create in your life, not on the faults of others.

The deeper meaning of this password can be understood as:

The only fault is in the thought that others are at fault. The world is a mirror and therefore, any deficiencies that you observe in the world are living projections of what is held within you. When

you apply this password, then your focus will be on looking within and cleansing.

In many ways, what you attract in your life are mirror images of your deficiencies. You may have never viewed the world as a mirror before, so let's look at this concept a bit closer.

If you're upset that you don't get help from others, it means in some area of your life, you're not helping yourself. If you find people are rude to you, then you need to look deeper at your relationships. This means you're being rude to yourself.

You've probably seen it in classrooms, or at least heard about it. A teacher complains that the students refuse to listen, they won't calm down and just about every other classic complaint about an unruly classroom.

Yet, when these same students enter the classroom of another teacher, they are the ideal of good behavior. There's not an unruly student in the group. The difference here is not how the students are, but how the teacher feels within herself. The first teacher is not committed to herself, so others, including her students, don't take her seriously. The second teacher listens to herself and because the world is a mirror, her students listen to her.

What happens in the outside world is a mirror of what is inside. When someone takes you for granted, it is a great opportunity for you to dive within and see where you take yourself for granted. Then stop taking yourself for granted. Change in the external world will automatically manifest as a result of the internal change.

You project your mental traits, unresolved emotions, and deficiencies upon the world. Therefore, what you see as the world is a reflection of what you project. People, situations, the weather - everything that you experience - are shaded by your perception and are projections of what is held deep within your mind.

You shape personalities for the people around you, by using building blocks present within your own mind. This happens on its own without your conscious awareness, and you end up criticizing people for shortcomings that are merely a projection of your own deficiencies. You experience your own unresolved emotions by unknowingly projecting them on people, so that it appears to you as though they are enacting or setting off those emotions.

You get lost in the external details to such an extent that you don't realize they are only living pictures of what lies buried within your mind. External situations are not the cause, but rather a reflection of what you hold within.

Different people react to the same situation in different ways - why is that so? It's because they are projecting or superimposing their own personal mental baggage on the same screen, and then watching the scene through their own personal mental filters that distort the picture of reality.

Let's say you're harboring anger within you. In this case, you can be sure that you'll see it in the external world and hold others as the reasons that you're angry. It could be, too, that you will see more anger in others. You'll view that people are unnecessarily angry toward you when it's not your fault.

Believe it or not, the true problem is not their anger toward you. It's the anger you have toward yourself. You are angry with yourself, so you perceive others as angry or as the cause of your anger.

Here's another example of how the universe is a mirror. Let's say your biggest complaint is that others aren't committed. In all probability if you look within you, you'll find an area where you're not committed to yourself. Lack of commitment then, is an issue from within you

There are leaders for whom people have an enormous amount of respect, love, and commitment. This is because they are committed to themselves, and commitment is a non-issue for them. As a result, they do not see a lack of commitment in others and automatically people are committed to them.

If you have understanding and awareness about this projection, you can use these situations to recognize what lies within you. You can open yourself to the possibility of clearing any distortions that exist in your perspective and raise yourself beyond the limitations of past conditioning.

The primary idea behind this password is that the world is a mirror, your thoughts should not be focused on the faults of others. If you want to wash your hands with soap, you must first remove the soap from its wrapper. Similarly, to attain your highest potential, you have to become free from your own despair and faults. For that, you must stop focusing on the faults of others, work within to improve yourself, and realize that whatever you see in the other person that is bothering you is actually your own reflection.

When resistance against something builds up within you or when you have constant complaints about something, immediately apply this password. Here is another example of how this can be used in your life.

If you are troubled by thoughts like, "I am so meticulous, but look at my wife and kids. All their things are scattered helter-skelter! Same is the case with my friends and relatives. They don't get any of their things in their place. Why can't they be disciplined like me? I detest people who are undisciplined and reckless."

It is great that you are meticulous and disciplined when it comes to keeping things in their place. The way to apply this password is to cleanse yourself from within instead of pointing out the fault in others.

Think about the areas of work where you're not meticulous. You may say, "I can't think of any place." But, think again, "Are you able to organize your thoughts in an appropriate place in the cupboard of your mind? Are you able to accomplish all your work as planned? Do you pay adequate attention to your health? Do you make right use of your wealth? Do you perform your social responsibilities well?"

When you really dig deep inside you, you'll notice that you may be neglecting your physical exercise and diet. Your mind is always enmeshed with several clashing thoughts. At times, you try to solve your office problems at home and other times, your personal, family problems at your workplace. You're not able to make optimal use of your wealth and try to escape and disregard your social responsibility, even when pressed for it by a familiar person.

When you're imperfect in so many areas of your life, why do you get angry over the few aspects where your children are imperfect? They are, in fact, serving as a mirror for you, showing you all those places where you are committing similar mistakes.

One day you'll open your eyes and say, "If my wife and kids, my friends and relatives are not behaving according to my expectations, instead of getting angry, I need to look deep within to see whether I'm behaving and living up to my expectations at all places."

When this happens, you need to sweep the negativity and the anger out of your mind. Replace it with, "I am organized when it comes to things, thoughts and my life. Everything is in its place in my life."

If you watch the sorrowful incidents of your life with the same old perspective, they'll bear the same old fruits that you have been getting until now. The meaning is clear – with the repetition of these events, you'll only suffer.

When you look at them through the eyes of wisdom, all the reasons for your suffering come to light one after another. The same events that were upsetting you, will become the cause of supreme bliss for you. You'll no longer feel as hurt and angry with people. When this happens, it will be a proof that the fifth password is successfully working in your life.

16

The Sixth Password to a Happy Life

As a society, we have a habit of either looking to the past or projecting into the future to find our happiness. For some people, they dwell in the good old days to recall how happy they were. Others, though, go chasing happiness hoping and wishing they'll find it in the future.

We know very few individuals who are happy wherever they are today. Even if they are happy, they tend to be careful not to say it too loudly. People look at you in disbelief why you're happy. Most of these people may not ask, even though they want to know your secret. Instead, they assume that you must be ignorant to be happy for no apparent reason.

You've many of your friends, no doubt, sigh and say, "When I get that promotion I'll be happy." Or "The only thing I need to be happy is a good spouse. Once I get married and start a household, I know I'll be happy."

By contrast, how many people do you hear say, "I'm happy right here and now. I am happy with whatever surrounds me right now."

Where does your happiness lie in all of this? Are you looking back seeing your happiness clearly in the rearview mirror? Or are you chasing happiness down the path knowing that it's in your future soon?

If your happiness has passed you by or you're waiting to meet it in the future, then consider what your present is worth. It's worth just pennies. The truth is the exact opposite.

The truth of the matter is that we all too readily become troubled when we think about the past or the future. Too often we feel distressed when we revisit our actions from the past. Similarly, when we think about the future, we're far too inclined to feel insecure when we think about what lies ahead of us.

When we do this, we lose the sense of this present moment.

The only way we can be truly happy is when we live in the present.

A person, who lives in the future, may think: "My marriage is still in a mess. Will I ever find my true love and get married? I'm not even near getting my ideal job, yet. What will happen in the future? I want to travel, but I don't see it happening."

All these negative thoughts about the past and the doubts about the future cloud the present. It does nothing but plunges these individuals into the dark abyss of suffering. This suffering then becomes a hurdle in their life.

When your mind runs haywire from the past to the future, remind yourself, **"It (whatever you're looking forward to) shall happen in the future and the future can occur anytime."**

This is the sixth password to a happy life which will bring you back into the present. This password implies – whatever is in the future will manifest – into the present at some time. When that happens, then we'll think about it.

This password can help you when you have thoughts similar to these, "This should happen. That should happen. Why isn't that happening?" The password will bring you back to the present. Let's look at an example of how this password can work.

You're at the bank waiting for your transaction to finish. It's taking longer than usual because the process of transferring money into your account is taking an unusually long time.

Use the password like this: "This thought that I should get my money is a thought regarding the future. I will get my money in the future. The future can happen at any time." If you do this, you'll find your resistance melting away.

Sometimes we get so worked up with the thoughts about what's going to happen in the future that we accidentally slip into depression. Some individuals even sink into such a low depression that they consider killing themselves. Their lives get beleaguered by suffering and despair, they don't even try to climb out of the abyss.

The key to true happiness is to learn to live in the present so you can receive those gifts that you want in your life and that are made especially for you. While you're living in the present, you'll need to learn how to sow positive seeds for your future. If you do this, you'll ensure a positive future. Don't allow those seeds of negativity. You'll only find negativity on your way to the future and you'll discover more weeds than flowers. And you'll find yourself facing nothing but suffering.

There's a kind of magic to this. And it is that your past only comes alive in the present, when you think about it. The same thing happens with the future. The future takes form and is born only from the present. This means that you must learn to live in the present.

The more time you spend in the present moment; it goes to figure that the happier you'll find yourself. Not only that, but when you live in the present, you'll be happier, right here and right now.

When you live in the present in happiness, you'll be sowing the seeds of happiness for the future. Once again, the present works its magic.

When you live in the present, happiness isn't the only aspect of your life that improves. You'll find yourself more prosperous, healthier, develop better relations, be more enthusiastic and more content.

So, what are the consequences of the wrong seeds? Suffering. When you sow the seeds of suffering, you'll find yourself walking around wondering what you're being punished for. If you inadvertently only think negatively at one point that you're only dwelling in the past or dreaming of the future, then you can naturally expect suffering.

If this is the case, then why do people sow the wrong seeds?

At those times when you find yourself living either in the past or the future, wallowing in sorrow, then this is the time to re-center yourself. Return to the present, by opening that door with the password, **"It shall happen in the future and the future can occur anytime."**

When you use the combination of planning and praying for the things you want, they'll start arriving in your life. You won't need to continue to keep thinking about them later.

Consider this: If you continue thinking about it on a daily basis, then you're not living in the present. If you've already taken the necessary action, then you don't need to revisit them. If you continue to dwell on them, day in and day out, then you're not living in the present.

You have sown the seeds of faith in your present. Have faith that whatever you desire will start coming on its own in your life. You must witness these miracles by living in the present.

The only way you can experience prosperity, contentment, pleasure, love, happiness and silence can be by living in the present. Therefore, exercise the sixth password in your life and start the practice of living in the present.

17

The Seventh Password to a Happy Life

Imagine this scenario. You're in a hurry and standing at an elevator waiting for it to stop at the floor you're on. You're cutting the time close, you know that. But if that elevator doesn't appear soon, you'll definitely be late for your meeting.

Your mind immediately starts talking to you, "I wonder what the problem with the elevator is? I hope the elevator is running fine and I'm not late. If there's something wrong with it, I'll be forced to use the staircase. The last time I was late for a meeting, my supervisor didn't take it well at all." With every ensuring negative thought, you experience more fatigue and worry.

This is the perfect time to use the seventh password to rescue yourself from scenarios that pull you deeper into depression. What's the seventh password? **"This is that."** It means: **This is that what I need.**

If the elevator doesn't show up, you'll say to yourself, "This is that." In the case of waiting for the elevator to appear, it means that this - waiting for the elevator - is what you need.

Believe it or not, the incessant chatter your mind has been putting you through will stop once you say this. Instead of vacillating between the past and the future, you'll find yourself remaining in the present. You'll experience a near immediate change in your perspective and your attitude. And you'll arrive at the meeting in a positive frame of mind.

Whatever you pray for gets fulfilled in a miraculous way, even if it doesn't seem like it to you at the time. When you pray for patience, then you'll find yourself in places that require patience. You'll be standing in an express line at a store that isn't moving. You'll be stuck in a traffic jam when you're running late for work or your toddler is extra inquisitive one day.

The caveat to this is that, at that moment, when you're waiting and waiting you might not remember that simple prayer. In fact, you may very well not accept this as your need. Your mind will argue with you and blame the others involved in the situation and attempt to postpone your happiness. Despite this, use the password, "This is that. This is that what I need. This is the situation I need."

When you exercise this help, you accept the situation. Understand that the situation is occurring as a result of your prayer. Your mind will then eventually calm down and you'll feel happy in that particular situation.

If you prayed for courage, you'll find yourself in circumstances where courage is demanded of you. It could be that you're placed in a situation that requires you to face something like a medical diagnosis. While you wait for the final word, waves of fear well up inside you.

Again, meet this circumstance affirming the password, "This is that. This incident has come to develop courage within me." You will then take up that situation as a challenge and soon you will find that you have the courage that you wanted.

Having understood this password for happiness, let's look into the causes of suffering – what causes unhappiness in the first place . . .

SECTION III
The Lock of Sorrow and Distress

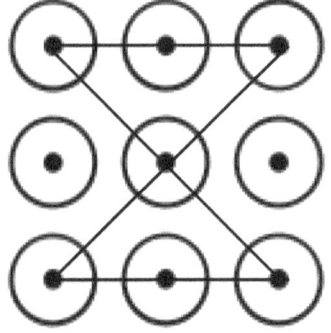

18

Cause 1: Separation from God

You could name any number of causes of suffering. But when you really take everything into account, you find that the ultimate cause is separation from God, leading to individuality.

If you contemplate on the above statement, you'll fully understand what this means. The first part of that sentence, "Separation from God," implies that you have temporarily forgotten that God, your higher Self, is your true essence. The word "individuality" in this scenario means that you identify with the body which you "assume" yourself to be – an individual who is separate from the rest of creation.

The word "God" used here doesn't refer to any image, figure or idol. It refers to the enlivening principle, the Source, Consciousness, Self, Self-experience, Self-witness, the Universal "I", which encompasses everyone and is also within each one. It refers to the One whose presence brings about the creation of this phenomenal cosmos.

When you forget your true nature, you invite suffering and endure it. When you forget your true identity, don't be surprised if things get confused and disordered. You may even want to call it chaotic

Thus, "Separation from God leading to creation of a false individual" is the beginning of suffering. Your first reason for suffering is within yourself. Instead of accepting this fact, you refuse to believe it.

Instead you insist that, "Someone else is the cause of my suffering." If you contemplate on this complaint, you'll realize the answer lies within your complaint itself. You are the cause of your own suffering.

Pure consciousness, that is to say pure love, is rooted in oneness. It knows no distinction or duality. Life naturally brings you the experiences of love, bliss, peace, health and harmony. Life naturally brings you vitality and abundance. When you experience this state of mind, nothing can negatively affect you, but your own beliefs, thoughts and emotions.

When you assume your limited body-mind as "I" you give birth to the illusion of "others." This, in turn, creates the delusion of emotions like anger, fear, greed, hatred, envy, ill-will and resentment.

When you entertain negative emotions in ignorance of your true nature, you give in to the illusion of separation. This action only causes you to resist the flow of life through your body. Negative, hurtful memories, bitterness, and ill-will choke the free flow of life within you.

When we resist the free flow of life, we experience testing circumstances, limitations and sorrow. Thoughts, feelings, words and actions that have arisen from the ignorant belief of separateness bind us and choke the expression of life.

Each of us creates his own story of suffering depending on his thoughts, which he considers to be correct. In ignorance, you invite all those individuals and circumstances which cause you suffering. These thoughts also fuel the suffering, like gasoline poured onto a fire. It accelerates the process. If that weren't enough, all of this then kick starts a vicious cycle of sorrow. Of course, you're not purposely seeking to be unhappy, it's just that you don't understand it out of ignorance, or at least temporarily forgot it.

In this way, you put yourself in a nearly inescapable, self-created web of suffering. You may never realize this and refuse to believe it if someone attempts to tell you what you're doing. Through spiritual understanding and meditation, you can shed this separation.

Having seen the first cause - the root cause, let's look at more causes.

19

Cause 2: The Habit of Dwelling in Sorrow

The second cause of your suffering is your habit of dwelling in sorrow.

You are so used to living side-by-side sorrow that you believe it to be a part and parcel of life and you refuse to come out of it. That's the reason you've suffered in the past and are still suffering even today.

Nature, by the way, never plans for us to suffer. It's not in nature's design to bring us sorrow and sadness. Nature's goal is to bring us happiness. You still suffer, despite this, because of your ignorance. When you gain wisdom, you realize that it's your own resistance, your refusal to accept the circumstances that is the true hurdle.

Think of happiness like a light. It's always around you. No one, however, has invented a button that can switch "on" darkness. Similarly, there is no switch to usher unhappiness. There's only one switch and that only brings happiness, it brings in light. Oh, sure, you may switch the button off to stop the flow of the light of happiness. You are the only person who can prevent happiness from entering your life. If you don't know this, though, you'll remain shrouded in the darkness of sorrow.

You're searching for happiness. But, if you look into the circumstances deeper, you'll realize that the experience of happiness is continuously occurring within you. Believe it or not, the wave of happiness is always passing through you like electricity. The reason you don't feel this is because you are used to switching that happiness button off. And this programming didn't just happen since you've become an adult. You've been programmed to do so since your childhood.

Because of this, you may helplessly continue to turn that switch of happiness off. It's like how a person can effortlessly reach out for a lamp, even in the dark and he's only half awake, can switch a lamp. That's because he knows exactly where the switch is. Similarly, when you don't realize the ultimate consequences of your actions, you switch that button of happiness off.

Nature never arranges for us to suffer. But man, due to his habit of dwelling in sorrow, does not wish to do anything to come out of it.

When you're asked to read a book to develop yourself in some way or attend a discourse, you'd bow to the habit of excusing yourself. Instead, you seek solace by watching your favorite TV shows. This is how you get into the habit of living with sorrow. Yes, you're really trying to take a break from this sorrow but you're not really ready to free yourself entirely from it. That's why you repeat the same answers over and over again.

Let's understand this further with the example of a policeman . . .

In the middle of the night, a wife tries to wake up her husband who's a police officer. She whispers in his ear, "There's some noise in the house. I think it's a robber who's broken in." Her husband refuses to take her concern seriously. "Go back to sleep. Don't bother me now. Can't you see I'm off duty."

What does this story tell you? The suspected intruder in this house is unhappiness. As soon as you know it's entering, you need to take immediate action. What type of action? Contemplation and introspection. Don't allow your mind to make any excuses. In every era, guidance has been offered to those who seek it and you too can be privy to this when you seek the truth.

Strengthen the power of your introspection

When Gautam Buddha encountered suffering, he didn't think, like the husband in the previous example. "Don't bother me now. Can't you see I'm not on duty." No, he handled the situation immediately by going deep within himself in contemplation. "Will I lead a life similar to others? Will I become sick one day? Will I die of old age?"

He may have also asked questions like these: "Is this what life is all about? This can't be it. There must be something beyond all of this?" As he contemplated, the intuition which he received from deep within was so powerful that it served as the guiding force in his quest for truth. His quest culminated in enlightenment.

Most of us never review our suffering from this perspective. But you should use your suffering to strengthen the truth. If lord Buddha could convert his suffering into a ladder for the attainment of truth, why can't we?

The reason we can't make the same assessment is because we are helplessly tied to our habits.

When you suffer, you don't look at ways to keep unhappiness away permanently. Instead, you prefer to be involved in mundane activities. Instead of doing serious soul-searching, you turn to TV programs, the internet, Facebook and other activities that aren't important. Instead of soul-searching, you assert that it's time to rest.

It's your time to go out and to shop or meet with friends. Or perhaps you forego looking within and open the daily paper. All of these things you do out of habit. Then at the same time you complain that you don't have the time to look into your suffering. After all, you're accustomed to living with sorrow and suffering. It's amazing what you can get used to and because of this you compulsively and ignorantly repeat it.

It's habit, pure and simple when all seems to be going well in a house, when out of the blue, some triggers a quarrel or teases someone. They come together to resolve the problem. To their credit, they devise a temporary solution. When this happens, they all go out to celebrate. The celebration gives them temporary relief which they misinterpret as happiness.

Do you see what is happening? You create your own suffering – the argument in the house – and then you find a solution to this suffering. But, as you are habitual of living with sorrow, you can't even think of living without the thought of suffering. Because of this, you continue to invite sorrow in for seemingly no reason at all.

You didn't develop this habit overnight. No, believe it or not you have gone to great lengths to train yourself to be unhappy. People all around you have taught you this. With this type of continuous training, it didn't take you long to get into the habit of being unhappy.

If you're serious about breaking this habit, how long do you think it will take you? Will it take 2,008 days . . . 1,008 days? Or do you think you can do it in 108 days? Believe it or not, you can do so in 108 days or even less.

Let's now look at one more cause of suffering...

20

Cause 3: Are we Unhappy about Others' Happiness?

"You appear gloomy today," Ed said to his friend Fred. "What's the matter?"

Fred simply replied, "England defeated Australia in the cricket match yesterday. I'm disappointed. I had a bet with my cousin that Australia would win, but boy I was wrong."

When a country loses a cricket match, its countrymen are naturally disappointed and even unhappy. And if on top of that they've lost a bet because of it . . . well, that only makes them even more upset. But, could there be another reason?

If you would honestly and seriously think about it, you'd realize that you're u**nhappy about someone's happiness.** Before you immediately disagree, think about it for a while.

Believe it or not, it really is the cause of your suffering. The fact that another person is happy makes you unhappy. Normally, we may not be unhappy when we lack some of the comforts of life. But the moment we see our neighbors enjoying these same comforts we become envious and unhappy. On a lighter note, if our neighbor's comforts and enjoyment are taken away, half of our suffering will disappear.

It seems to be a universal law, that **what you envy in another's life, you won't receive it in yours.** If you envy at the happiness of others, you'll never see happiness in your life. But, when you rejoice to see others happy, then you'll receive happiness in your life as well. To truly understand this, let's look at an example.

One morning, Mr. Green started his walk to work, when a bull charged at him. This happened more than once. He finally started wondering, "The bull doesn't follow me when I go out on some other errand. But whenever I go out to earn money, it invariably chases me. Why?" At long last, he did some self-introspection and realized that his own thoughts were the root cause for this strange occurrence.

So how did Mr. Green finally think this through? He realized that whenever he was on his way to work, his mind inevitably wandered to thoughts like this, "My neighbor has bought a car, but I can't even afford a scooter. The neighbor on the other side of me has built a new house that looks more like a mansion, but look at my home. All I could afford to build was a small cottage. My neighbor frequently has rich and elite visitors, but no one comes to see me."

Whenever Mr. Green was green with envy, he turned red with hatred and anger. Now, it's a known fact that bulls charge at the sight of red. Thus, the root cause lied in his own thoughts which instigated the bull.

Sure, when you're not aware of what you're doing, you envy someone else's happiness and in turn that envy prevents you from feeling happy. Your envy blocks the happiness in your own life. This is why you must burn the envy with the fire of understanding.

The button that prevents joy from entering your life at this time is because of the envy you have for the other individual. **The day you learn the habit of truly experiencing happiness for your friend's good fortune is the day you'll begin to see joy boundlessly entering your life and happiness rising in leaps and bounds around you.**

When you envy others, you become a "non-magnet." You'll never be able to attract the good things you want. That's reason enough that should make you consider eliminating all envy. This probably won't be easy. Envy has long roots and once it has dug into you, it's hard to get rid of. Let's rewind the previous conversation. When you see your neighbor prospering, you'll find yourself saying, "My neighbor has a car, a beautiful bungalow. I'm very happy to see him doing well."

But you must say this sincerely. If you say this and still harbor jealously, then you'll remain a non-magnet to the good things in life. Merely saying the words without meaning them won't bring you the happiness you're looking for.

You'll only feel happiness when you genuinely feel for the welfare of those around you. When you learn this, happiness won't be a stranger.

Your first step is to focus on happiness. As you very well know whatever you focus on, you attract into your life. If you refuse to acknowledge the happiness surrounding you on all sides, how can you expect to attract it into your life? There's the missing link. When you focus on a particular object with happiness, you attract happiness into your life. But, the opposite is also true. If you focus on an object with a sad feeling, you'll do nothing but place obstacles in your path toward happiness. And happiness then can't reach you.

It's also a law of nature that whatever you focus on with that same sad feeling, won't be attracted to you. Think about this. If you view the simple joys of life through the lens of unhappiness, these joys will continue to elude you.

To be joyful, you need to see the joys of life from the viewpoint of happiness. You'll start experiencing the law of happiness, the moment you show genuine joy for the happiness of others. Start looking at the joys of life, yours or your neighbors, or your friends or relatives. If you can say you feel joy for even the happiness of a complete stranger, you're on a powerful step toward attracting happiness to you.

Develop the habit of examining all the good things happening in your vicinity. Even while watching TV serials, pay attention to happy characters. It is true that you will find very few happy characters in TV soaps; but pay attention to as many as you can find.

Without harboring any hatred in your mind, if you focus only on happy people, you'll attract happiness into your life. The simplest secret of being happy is – **See great everywhere. "See Great" is the Secret.**

Whenever you get time, focus on all the good things happening around you. In this way, feel the happiness that people around you are experiencing. When you entertain happy thoughts for others, when you pray for their wellbeing, then happiness will come racing into your life.

Change your negative thinking

Because of jealousy, envy and general negative thinking, you'll find unwanted things creeping into your life. The process is so gradual that you remain completely unaware of them. You'll wonder what's happening and ask yourself, "I never thought ill of others, then why do bad things happen to me?"

You don't realize that these negative situations are not attracted into your life overnight, even though it feels as if you wake up one morning realizing this. No, rather you've been thinking these thoughts or similar ones for years through your continual focusing on the negative aspect of, well everything. As a result, you now find yourself unable to rejoice in others' happiness. Not only that, but your own flow of happiness gets clogged, it dries up. You realize this only if you understand how vital it is to remain happy in all situations. If this were the case, then you wouldn't have entertained envious thoughts for others.

It's a powerful power of grace when we see and appreciate happiness in others. If you are not capable of seeing others' happiness and instead get upset, then you'll find it impossible to attract happiness into your life. We all know people who love to make doomsday predictions, choosing to believe the earth will end on a certain day. These people need to be told that the earth has never been short of happy people, so there's no chance of any possibility of the earth ending.

You need to develop this understanding within you that you should look at the joys of the other people through the lens of happiness. At the same time, whenever you encounter unhappy people, remind them about all the good things that they are already blessed with, which they should feel happy about. Often man disregards what he already has and laments for that which he does not have. From now onwards, make it your duty to remind everyone about their good qualities, abilities, expertise, uniqueness and achievements.

This understanding that you should rejoice in happiness of others is enough to be happy. If you understand this principle of nature, you'll always remain happy. You won't postpone your happiness due to reasons like, "First let me accomplish this task. Let me get married. Let a baby boy be born. Let me have a house. Let me own a car. Let my birthday or the new year arrive… then I will be happy."

When you learn to use this password of happiness, you won't wait for any happy event to make you happy. Instead, you'll always stay happy.

21

Cause 4: Feeling Unhappy about Unhappiness

The fourth cause of unhappiness is being unhappy about your unhappiness.

It's like adding insult to injury. It's bad enough that you're not happy. Then you experience contrition and sorrow because you know you should be happy but you're not. You can think of this as "double unhappiness" if you like. And what you may not have known is this double unhappiness is the large cause of unhappiness for most people.

It's much easier to explain it with an example than to talk in circles about it. Let's say your body is aching. This would naturally cause unhappiness in most people. So, you can say that the pain triggers the original unhappiness. Your mind then questions what's happening.

"Why am I in pain? Why me? When will this pain settle down." It's when the mind refuses to accept the lack of feeling good is the point at which your double unhappiness begins.

Yes, your body may be in pain, but despite this, you know that at the very same time, your body is busily healing itself. Part of the problem is that you adopted the pain as your own using the words "my pain," as so many people do. You've probably used the phrase "my unhappiness." This type of language only multiplies your pain and instead of working on curing yourself, you're inadvertently doubling your unhappiness.

You've seen this scenario play out over and over again, especially with children. One minute the children are angry. But then in a few minutes you see them playing peacefully again. The anger has passed, there's no remorse and they have forgotten all about it.

Now compare this situation to your anger. It doesn't trouble in that moment. The episode is over. But, the problem is your mind is still thinking about it, mulling it over. The episode may be over but the thoughts you have about it that provides a continuance of the anger.

As your understanding of this process increases, you begin to rid yourself of the double unhappiness. Remember that unhappiness in and of itself doesn't possess the capacity to trouble you.

Now, we can look at these circumstances in this light: non-acceptance is unhappiness; acceptance is happiness. So, what's the lesson here? Simply to accept those moments of unhappiness, don't resist it at the time and then let the episode go. After all, it's over.

And it's really not as difficult as you may think it is. Simply ask yourself this one question, "Can I accept this?" In most cases, you will be able to accept the unhappiness.

Of course, there'll be a circumstance or two where you just can't seem to accept it or let it go. What should you do in those rare moments. That's when you ask this question: "Can I accept that I cannot accept this unhappiness?"

This is not just a play of words. Accepting the fact that your unhappiness is bothering you, perhaps even gnawing at you is important. Then once you can do this, let it go. When you acknowledge this, you'll find you're back on the road to happiness.

It doesn't really matter how large or small the episode appears in your life. What is true at one level is true at all levels. You may think that this is just a small step. But when you do so, it causes a giant shift in your consciousness. At that very moment, you open up a wonderful realm you may never have experienced before and you begin to attract more positive things.

Even the smallest "letting- go" action positively affects every facet of your life. Not only do you become mentally free, but it affects you at the physical, emotional, social and financial levels, setting off a chain reaction that reverberates through your entire being and leaves you in quite a different place than you were before.

Safeguard yourself from an ignorant ego

The main reason for double unhappiness is because of your individual ego. It's borne out of ignorance. At the end of every incident, it's human nature to assess it with this "ignorance." What happens is the ego gets hurt and you suffer. When you consider yourself to be your body, it's only natural to view pain as suffering. You immediately think, "Either somebody or something externally is causing my suffering."

But you can end this vicious circle by honestly asking yourself, "Why am I feeling negative? Am I feeling hurt because someone swore at me? Do I feel unhappy only when these particular swear-words are used or do I get upset regardless of these words?"

If you perform a post-mortem after every incident, you'll be able to pinpoint the root cause of your unhappiness. You can be rest assured that the answer you'll receive will be exactly the opposite of what you had thought about.

Break free from your old recording with the help of right understanding

If you reflect deeply enough, you'll know that you're associating a belief with every word. You connect a feeling with every word. You find yourself in this position based on experiences you've been through which get recorded in your memory.

If you were to investigate every situation like this, you'll discover that a painful feeling arises with every bad word you hear. Hearing these words triggers the feelings associated with them. It's like all the old tapes which had been recorded in the past are replayed in your mind again and you begin to feel unhappy.

If you expect to be happy even in these situations, then you must stop playing those recordings. And you can do this with the help of the right understanding. You don't just need to quit playing those recordings but you have to replace those recordings with an entire set of new ones. You'll be able to do this once you have thought of several new recordings you can use upon demand. One of the best ways is to associate these "bad words" with something that will make you laugh.

Then when no negative feelings develop after you hear these words, then you can say with confidence, "Now, I'm free from the unhappiness. It doesn't negatively affect me any longer. I've been successful in replacing the file."

So, what does this mean for you?

This creates an opportunity for you to achieve your real goal on earth. When you create new upbeat files, you open up a realm of happiness, as well as prosperity. Once you do this, the sky's the limit.

Just go through whatever unhappiness you are faced with, not more than that.

You'll inevitably be hit with certain circumstances where you'll find that you're sad. In instances like these make an agreement with yourself that you'll allow yourself to feel badly for, let's say, two minutes. But only two minutes. Keep that as a strict deadline. After that, you go back to your normal routine.

When sadness and sorrow strike, ask yourself this, "How deep is this pain and how long should I be sad and upset over it?" When you decide on your answer, then act accordingly. If you don't think the two minutes mentioned above isn't enough, then make the sorrowful time-out half an hour, an hour, one day, two days… You set the time limit. Then, make sure you tell your family about it. Follow the lead of those who fast. The person informs his family so no one offers him food.

Everyone will understand and will only speak to you if it's absolutely necessary. Once your time limit is over, you'll discover that you'll be refreshed and enthusiastic. You'll have no trouble making right decisions. But the biggest asset to all of this is you've shed your sadness.

Consider this next statement carefully. You can stay happy around-the-clock for an entire 365 days a year.

First, though, you need to rise above your current level of entanglement. If you don't learn how to do this, then you won't succeed. In fact, you may even find it difficult to stay happy for even one day.

But don't aim too high too soon. Small successful beginnings are more important than large failed ones. So, start by only taking a few steps. But, only endure that suffering that you can't avoid and no more.

Look at it this way, even if you're not happy for some of the days out of year, that means you'll be happy the rest of the days. Celebrate in that gain. Think about the benefits of being happy even one third of the days in a year. Otherwise, you'll take on more suffering than you need to. You may find that out of 365 days, you're only happy for eight to ten days, for a few days during holidays and festivals. So wise up and don't take on more sorrow than you need to.

This may surprise you, but there are many people who have retained their happiness every day of the year. These are people, who have attained Self-realization. The bodies where the Self is realized, open to some novel, unique and divine secrets. People in such a state become completely free from suffering and lead their lives happily. This state can be attained in every human being, simply because this is the sole factual truth of life.

22

Cause 5: Forgetting the True Purpose of Life

Just making a career, earning money, getting married, rearing children, helping those children make their careers, bringing up their children, and then passing away is not the mission on earth. Along with these activities, if you're not engaged in making your mind steadfast, obedient, untainted and loving, then you'll depart from this world, having lived a life full of unhappiness, without achieving your sole purpose.

Our sole purpose is actually the SOUL purpose where SOUL is an acronym which can be expanded as -

S - Steadfast, which means making the mind unshakable under all circumstances.

O - Obedient, means making the mind obedient and completely harmonized.

U - Untainted, in other words, making the mind pure by removing the filth of hatred.

L - Loving, implies making the mind unconditionally loving towards all.

Thus, training our mind to attain the SOUL purpose is the real purpose of life on Earth.

Begin embracing your SOUL purpose as your mission today. Train your mind by focusing on the virtues of people and develop those good qualities in you. Then, truthfulness will become your virtue, and virtuousness will become your truth.

When you focus your attention completely on the SOUL purpose, you'll not only free yourself from unhappiness and dissatisfaction, but you'll also help others shed their dissatisfaction.

But, first things first. That means you need to focus your attention on your goal. If you become distracted from that mission, you'll experience unhappiness in life.

You can understand this better with an example. When parents take their children to the garden to play, they're content watching them play. But when their attention shifts from the children to the filth and dirt around, they get upset. Likewise, when man shifts his focus away from his goal, he becomes discontent. Therefore, always keep your focus on your goal. When you become free from unhappiness, you help others get rid of unhappiness.

As you make your mind pure, you'll automatically become a magnet for happiness. You encounter many incidents in your everyday life that provide you with an opportunity to make your mind unshaken, pure and loving. Here's an example of what it means.

When you see water in a water tank from above, it may appear sparkling clean. However, when you stir up the water, all the dirt settled at the bottom of the tank will come to surface, giving the water a muddled appearance. It's then that you realize that the water was indeed dirty to begin with. In order to make the water clean, you need to remove the dirt from it. Only then in a true sense, the water can be called pure.

When your life goes smoothly without any incidents, it's a lot like that water tank. It appears to be pure. With nothing to disturb your mind, the dirt remains hidden deep within your mind. This may cause you to announce that, "There's no impurity in my mind. My mind is pure." But you're in a great illusion. Don't live in such deception and ignore the dirt that's settled at the bottom. During the storm of unhappy incidents, all the dirt will come to light. Instead, make use of everyday incidents as opportunities to purify your mind.

Your purpose of coming into this world is to shed yourself of these impurities. We all have been given opportunity to do this. A quarter of your life, in fact, is time enough to do this. Think about this, we've been granted a life four times the length needed to get rid of our impurities.

So why does it not seem like it's enough time?

That's because we don't make it a priority, so we fail to work at it. This isn't due so much to neglect, but to a lack of understanding on our part. We need to train our minds to be steadfast, obedient, untainted and loving.

Have a foresight, achieve your goal

A mind trained on your SOUL purpose is your greatest asset. Everything pales in comparison to this. Those individuals who have attained this achievement can call themselves truly successful. The world isn't going to praise you and you'll not gain celebrity status, and you won't be guaranteed the luxuries of the world.

All of that shows why many individuals aren't motivated to achieve their purpose merely by a cursory look. Only those who are farsighted realize that training for your SOUL purpose is the only thing that matters in the long term.

It's difficult for many individuals to believe in matters like this. It's much easier to believe in those things directly visible. But to see and believe that which is unseen very often requires a spiritual guide, a guru. The ability of our mind can handle that which we see with our eyes and other senses. But, a spiritual guide, your guru raises your foresight as well as your receptivity for the more subtler aspects. With his help you'll be able to see how the unseen world works as well.

Think about this for a moment. You suffer for good reason at all because you can't see the unseen. You haven't come into the world to be president. But yet you become one. If you haven't found your SOUL purpose, you'll be the world's unhappiest president.

You're designed to constantly receive feedback in the form of your feelings which get triggered in good times as well as bad times. When you get pleasant feelings while you're doing something, just be sure that you're doing something for which you've come to earth to do.

That's why you need to vow that you're not going to leave this world before you achieve your SOUL purpose. Keep in mind that you can cultivate virtuous habits just as easily as adopting vices. Vow that you'll develop a habit that will lead you to attain this goal. When you do this, you'll be surprised how easy it can be.

23

Cause 6: Actions backed by Ignorance

Once, a postman had to travel a long distance to deliver a letter to a villager. While handing over the letter, the postman grumbled, "I had to walk four kilometers to reach this place, just to deliver it to you."

The illiterate villager replied, "Why did you go through so much trouble? You should have just dropped the letter in the postbox nearby. It would have reached me."

The villager didn't understand. That's why it's said, "There's no limit to what ignorance can make you think." When a person is unaware he always wonders, "This could have happened or probably that could have taken place." Whatever he says only reflects his ignorance. That's why it's important to rid yourself of any ignorance before discovering your happiness.

You'll continue to encounter suffering when your actions spring from unawareness or ignorance. **The sixth reason for man's suffering is – actions backed by ignorance.** The example of the postman illustrates this.

What exactly can eliminate ignorance? The light of wisdom alone is able to dispel the darkness of ignorance. You need to ensure that your actions are based on wisdom. Actions springing from wisdom have a devotion in them. Devotion is permeated with happiness. When your actions are backed with wisdom they embrace the three royal paths: that of wisdom, devotion and action.

Such actions arise from the melding of skill, discernment and intelligence. Before you do anything, always assess whether the actions you take come from the proper understanding of the truth or from blind devotion as well as unawareness of the possible outcome of the action.

It doesn't matter whether the action seems correct for those watching from the outside. The true test is to determine that the action is backed by wisdom or ignorance. The example below illustrates this well.

A man's house caught fire. His neighbor noticed the fire blazing and shouted at him, "How can you sit so patiently when your house is on fire? Why aren't you doing anything?" The man quietly replied, "Of course I am praying to God for the rains."

This is blind devotion in action. This example shows that the man lacked not only understanding but also discerning power. The circumstances demanded that he should have been taking immediate steps to put the fire out. But because you take actions doesn't mean that you can't also pray at the same time.

While you're praying, you should also be performing insightful actions. The man in the illustration only prayed for rains out of ignorance or unawareness. Had he started to put out the fire, you could probably guess what would have happened next. Neighbors would have flocked to him to help.

You need the proper understanding in order to respond most appropriately regardless of the situation. One way to say it is that you should respond with devotion. Doing so, all of your tasks will happen effortlessly. But that's not all, your action becomes devotion and in turn love becomes your nature.

Devotion is an integral part of actions backed by proper understanding. If devotion were to be taken away from your life, you'll discover that along with it went happiness. Devotion is every bit as important as wisdom. Why? Because it's directly connected to your feelings. And feelings are closer to the heart. And it's only through your heart that you can experience the bliss of Self-realization.

Actions based on this higher understanding are just that. With a higher understanding you don't need to worry what to do next, you'll know. You won't have to worry about what to say next, it will flow from your heart and out of your mouth. If thinking is required, the proper contemplation takes place. You automatically provide an appropriate response depending on what the situation requires.

There are some individuals who like to act as if they are intellectually superior to the rest. They brag that they take no action when it's required. They hide their lethargy and apathy behind beautiful words of wisdom.

But the moment you ask them to do something, they will impress upon you with logical reasons backed by their wisdom, only to conclude at the end of it that no action needs to be taken. They talk more than they need to in order to influence you with their worthiness. And most of all, you can hear them saying things like, "This is not right. This should not happen" in support of their reasoning.

Then there are other individuals who safeguard themselves from mistakes by avoiding taking action by making wonderful excuses. They're great at giving advice but think before you accept it. It's provided out of ignorance and more often than not yields no results. Their unnecessary talk won't solve anything. This is another action created out of ignorance. Your actions must also arise from wisdom.

When you act with wisdom, the feeling of devotion will increase within you, everything you do will then become an expression of the Self. The expression of true devotion will only yield bliss.

People become unhappy as a result of actions performed out of ignorance. They provide you with empty arguments and lame excuses in a frantic attempt to escape their problems. This may give them a temporary feeling of ease, but the problem still persists. The only way to dispel the darkness of ignorance is with the light of wisdom. You must stop performing actions that stem from a shroud of ignorance. It's so much easier to free yourself from these actions. Make your goal to ensure each of your actions is backed with wisdom.

24

Cause 7: The Restlessness of the Mind

Instead of living in the present, we live in the future or the past.

Have you ever caught yourself doing that? You believe something wonderful happens tomorrow so you keep waiting for tomorrow to arrive. That's all well and good. But by doing this do you realize what you've just done?

You've surrendered your "today." You've given away your chance to be happy today.

When people do this, they vacillate between the worries of the past and the anxieties of the future. But they're also doing one more thing, they open the door and invite sorrow in their hearts. But that's not all. It's very likely that they also postpone many of their tasks. They just don't seem to have the energy for them.

If you learn, instead, to remain in the present moment and put it to good, effective use then it brings you happiness. Living in the past, living in the future is unhappiness. Living in the present is happiness. And the best way to use your time wisely is to exercise the right and proper understanding.

The seventh reason for man's suffering is the churning of the mind.

As an example, there are many festivals and holidays during the year, whether it's Christmas, Eid or Diwali. On each festival, there's always someone who says, "Last year Diwali was splendid; this year it's not much fun. Last year, Christmas was wonderful; this year it's cold and dull." In this way, he always dwells in the past. Every festive occasion, never quite lives up to last year's celebrations. In those moments, they're living in the past and it doesn't live up, according to them to the present. Because of this habit, they never experience joy in the present moment.

You've probably noticed that when students return home from school on Saturday, they're exceptionally happy. They dance and jump around in joy. Although the school has a holiday on Sunday, the students, in anticipation of their holiday, enjoy more on a Saturday than on a Sunday. This is because while returning from school on Saturday, they think, "Tomorrow is Sunday. It's a holiday. We will have fun tomorrow." But on Sunday, they think, "Tomorrow is Monday. I have to go back to school tomorrow morning."

The "Monday syndrome" is actually the mind syndrome. The faculty of the mind which constantly chatters, weighs, compares, judges and labels everything is the culprit. It's the cause of unhappiness. This is referred to as the contrast mind. The ceaseless commentary of the contrast mind is nothing less than a disease.

The contrast mind never remains in the present. It always jumps either in the past or in the future. When you can see the contrast mind for what it is, when you're able to clearly see through its mischief, you'll be able to come out of that unhappiness.

When you refuse to be deluded by the past or anxious about the future, you rid yourself of the cause of unhappiness and sorrow. You remain happy only by being in the present. Thus, you should destroy ignorance and hatred with the fire of higher understanding.

Live or fight

When man arrives on this plane, in this visible world, he burns the bridge behind. He can't leave Earth for several years. It's like in ancient times when the military would charge while in battle, once the soldiers reached across the border, they would burn the back bridge behind to the kingdom, so that no soldier would retreat due to fear. They were left with only two choices – Fight or Die. Likewise, obtaining a human body is like burning the back bridge.

Once the bridge is burnt, those of us in this world are left with two choices: Fight or Live. The problem is far too many of us only remember the words, "Fight or Die" and either forget or ignore the "Living" part. Those people who have suicidal thoughts must understand they've burnt the back bridge and must fight.

The word fighting when used in this sense doesn't imply a fight with any army, but the fight is between understanding and your agitated mind. It's not about using a sword but relying on your understanding. You must make use of your sword of discretion and armor of understanding.

When you will fight with the sword of discretion, you'll live life by being life.

If you fail to make use of your higher understanding, your life will be full of thoughts about the past and the future, incessant constant chatter of the mind and confusion of several problems. When you stop making proper use of your past and future, you stop living in the present.

You should make use of time and not allow time to make use of you. If you're unable to live in the present, it means that time is making use of you.

Suffering automatically creates a strong longing for freedom. When Lord Buddha encountered intense suffering, he wholeheartedly resolved, "This is enough. Now, I must witness the state of liberation." This feeling of longing for freedom from suffering was so profound in him that actions leading to search for truth automatically happened through him. Actions are the result of feelings. The prayers that emanate from you automatically lead to suitable actions and you reach your ultimate goal.

You can send your opinion or feedback on this book to :

Tej Gyan Foundation, Pimpri Colony, P. O. Box 25, Pimpri, Pune – 411017 (Maharashtra), INDIA.
Email : mail@tejgyan.com

About Sirshree

(Symbol of Acceptance)

Sirshree's spiritual quest which began during his childhood, led him on a journey through various schools of thought and meditation practices. His overpowering desire to attain the truth made him relinquish his teaching job. After a long period of contemplation, his spiritual quest culminated in the attainment of the ultimate truth. Sirshree says, **"All paths that lead to the truth begin differently, but end in the same way—with understanding. Understanding is the whole thing. Listening to this understanding is enough to attain the truth."**

Sirshree is the author of several spiritual books. His books have been translated in more than 10 languages and published by leading publishers such as Penguin and Hay House. He is the founder of Tej Gyan Foundation, a not-for-profit organization committed to raising mass consciousness by spreading "Happy Thoughts" with branches in the United States, India, Europe and Asia-Pacific. Sirshree's retreats have transformed the lives of thousands and his teachings have inspired various social initiatives for raising global consciousness.

His works include more than 100 books and 3000 discourses. Various luminaries and celebrities such as His Holiness the Dalai Lama, publishers Mr. Reid Tracy and Ms. Tami Simon and yoga master Dr. B. K. S Iyengar have released Sirshree's books and lauded his work. 'The Source' book series, authored by Sirshree, has sold more than 10 million copies in 5 years. His book *The Warrior's Mirror*, published by Penguin, was featured in the Limca Book of Records for being released on the same day in 11 languages.

Tejgyan... The Road Ahead

What is Tejgyan?

Tejgyan is the existential wisdom of the ultimate truth, which is beyond duality. In today's world, there are a lot of people who feel disharmony and are desperately trying to achieve some balance in an unpredictable life. Tejgyan helps them in harmonizing with their true nature, the Self, thereby restoring balance in all aspects of their life.

And then there are those who are successful but feel a sense of emptiness or void within. Tejgyan provides them fulfillment and helps them to embark on a journey towards self-realization. There are others who feel lost and are seeking the meaning of life. Tejgyan helps them to realize the true purpose of human life.

All this is possible with Tejgyan due to a very simple reason. The experience of the ultimate truth is always available. The direct experience of this truth or self-realization is possible provided the right method is known. Tejgyan is that method, that understanding. At Tej Gyan Foundation, Sirshree imparts this understanding through a System for Wisdom – a series of retreats that guides participants step by step

Magic of Awakening Retreat

Magic of Awakening is the flagship self-realization retreat offered by Tej Gyan Foundation where participants gain access to the experience of the Self and learn to live in the present every moment. The retreat is conducted in two languages – Hindi and English. The teachings of the retreat are non-denominational (secular).

Participate in the *Magic of Awakening* retreat to attain the ageless wisdom through a unique and simple 'System for Wisdom' so that you can:

1. Live from pure and still presence allowing the natural qualities of consciousness, viz. peace, love, joy, compassion, abundance and creativity to manifest.

2. Acquire simple tools to use in everyday life which help quieten the chattering mind, revealing your true nature.

3. Get practical techniques to gain access to pure presence at will and connect to the source of all answers (the inner guru).

4. Discover the missing links in the practices of meditation *(dhyana)*, action *(karma)*, wisdom *(gyana)* and devotion *(bhakti)*.

5. Understand the nature of your body-mind mechanism to attain freedom from tendencies and patterns.

6. Learn practical methods to shift from mind-centred living to consciousness-centred living.

This residential retreat is held for 3-5 days at the foundation's MaNaN Ashram amidst the glory of mountains and the pristine beauty of nature. This ashram is located at the outskirts of the city of Pune in India, and is well connected by air, road and rail. The retreat is also held at other centres of Tej Gyan Foundation across the world.

For retreats contact +919921008060 or email: mail@tejgyan.com

A Mini retreat is also conducted, especially for teens (14-17 years) during summer and winter vacations.

Register online for all the above retreats at www.tejgyan.org

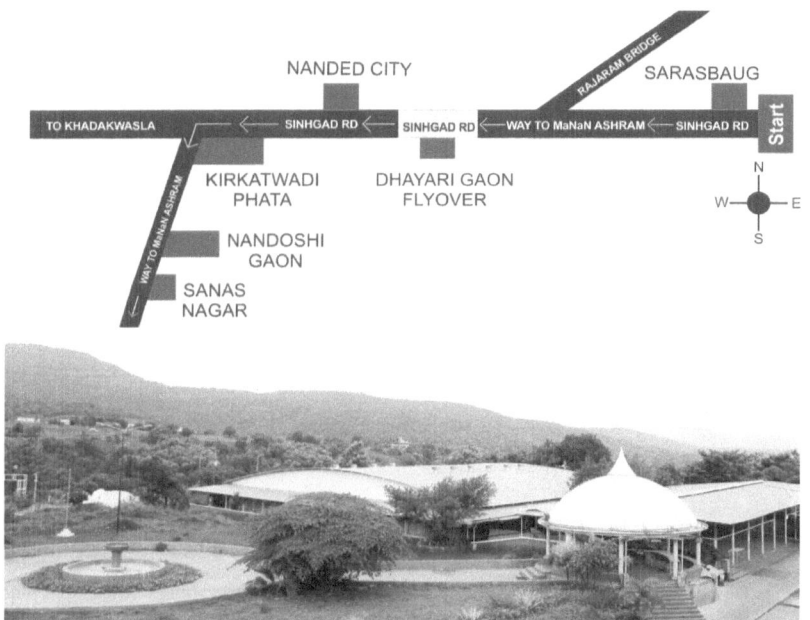

MaNaN Ashram :

Survey No. 43, Sanas Nagar, Nandoshi gaon, Kirkatwadi Phata, Sinhagad Road, Tal. Haveli, Dist. Pune 411024, Maharashtra, India. Contact No.: 992100 8060.

About Tej Gyan Foundation

Tej Gyan Foundation (TGF) was established with the mission of creating a highly evolved society through all-round self development of every individual that transforms all the facets of his/her life. It is a non-profit organization founded on the teachings of Sirshree. The foundation has received the ISO certification (ISO 9001:2008) for its system of imparting wisdom. It has centres all across India as well as in other countries. The motto of Tej Gyan Foundation is 'Happy Thoughts'.

TGF is creating a highly evolved society through:

- Tejgyan Programs (Retreats, Courses, Television and Radio Programs, Podcasts)

- Tejgyan Products (Books, Tapes, Audio/Video CDs)

- Tejgyan Projects (Value Education, Women Empowerment, Peace Initiatives)

The foundation undertakes various projects to elevate the level of consciousness among school students, youth, women, senior citizens, teachers, doctors, leaders, organizations, police force, prisoners, etc.

Now you can register **online** for the following retreats

Maha Aasmani Niwasi Shivir
(5 Days Residential Retreat in Hindi)

Magic of Awakening Retreat
(3 Days Residential Retreat In English)

Mini Maha Aasmani Shivir
3 Days (Residential) Retreat for Teens

🔍 www.tejgyan.org

Books can be delivered at your doorstep by registered post or courier. You can request for the same through postal money order or pay by VPP. Please send the money order to either of the following two addresses:

WOW Publishings Pvt. Ltd.

1. Registered Office: E-4, Vaibhav Nagar, Near Tapovan Mandir, Pimpri, Pune 411017.

2. Post Box No. 36, Pimpri Colony Post Office, Pimpri, , Pune 411017
Phone No. : 9011013210 / 9623457873
YOU CAN ALSO ORDER YOUR COPY AT THE ONLINE STORE:
Log in at: www.gethappythoughts.org
*Free Shipping plus 10% Discount on purchases above Rs. 300/-.

Other Related Books by Sirshree

You are Meditation

Discover Peace and Bliss within

ISBN:

978-81-8322-786-5

Total Pages: 148

Manjul Publishing House Pvt.Ltd.

Starting with the basics, this book will guide you towards the ultimate goal of meditation where you dissolve into the silent stillness of pure consciousness and realize that you are meditation – your true nature of love, bliss and peace. The book demystifies meditation by examining both its superficial and its most profound benefits. It elaborates the training and practice needed to master the body–mind.

Mind Your Brain Master Your Life

Practical Methods to Create Healthy Pathways in your Brain

ISBN:

978-81-8415-641-6

Total Pages: 128

WOW Publishings Pvt. Ltd.

New discoveries in brain research have shown that our brain can be re-wired through Neuroplasticity. This book will be helpful for those who want to mold their brain to unleash their infinite possibilities. It systematically throws light on brain research, practical applications of brain re-wiring and spiritual insights in various areas. The simple techniques given in this book, if applied correctly, can bring about a radical transformation in your life. Your life can be filled with love, bliss, peace, health, prosperity and contentment.

ISBN:
978-81-8415-410-8

Total Pages: 190

WOW Publishings Pvt.Ltd.

Everything is a Game of Beliefs

Understanding is the Whole Thing

This book is an eye-opener to the myths and superstitions we have acquired so far. It helps you bring out the beliefs that you have been holding onto. In the bright light of understanding, you can discover their reality and transcend them. This book covers myths related to topics like time, money, success, confidence, love, marriage, death, and divinity. It also covers everyday superstitions we believe in.

ISBN:
978-81-8415-494-8

Total Pages: 168

WOW Publishings Pvt.Ltd.

Who am I Now

Beyond mindfulness into no-mind

Presented in a simple Q/A format, this book provides all the missing links and knowledge of Self, which helps to reach your true self, easily and definitively. "Who am I?" is the question asked in Self Enquiry that will lead you to the experience of the Self. While "Who am I Now?" is a new and unique method presented in this book that will help you stay in that experience, in and through your daily affairs. This will dismantle the daydream of who you believe yourself to be and enable you to get established in the experience of pure consciousness.

For further details contact:

Tejgyan Global Foundation

Registered Office:
Happy Thoughts Building, Vikrant Complex, Near Tapovan Mandir, Pimpri, Pune 411017, Maharashtra, India.
Contact No: 020-27411240, 27412576
Email: mail@tejgyan.com

MaNaN Ashram:
Survey No. 43, Sanas Nagar, Nandoshi gaon, Kirkatwadi Phata, Sinhagad Road, Tal. Haveli, Dist. Pune 411024, Maharashtra, India.
Contact No: 992100 8060.

Hyderabad: 9885558100, **Bangalore:** 9880412588,

Delhi: 9891059875, **Nashik:** 9326967980, **Mumbai:** 9373440985

For accessing our unique 'System for Wisdom' from self-help to self-realization, please follow us on:

	Website	www.tejgyan.org
	Video Channel	www.youtube.com/tejgyan For Q&A videos: http://goo.gl/YA81DQ
	Social networking	www.facebook.com/tejgyan
	Social networking	www.twitter.com/sirshree
	Internet Radio	http://www.tejgyan.org internetradio.aspx

Online Shopping
www.gethappythoughts.org

Pray for World Peace along with thousands of others at 09:09 a.m. and p.m. every day

www.ingramcontent.com/pod-product-compliance
Lightning Source LLC
LaVergne TN
LVHW041849070526
838199LV00045BB/1517